Quick Guide to

Digital Audio Recording

Ian Waugh

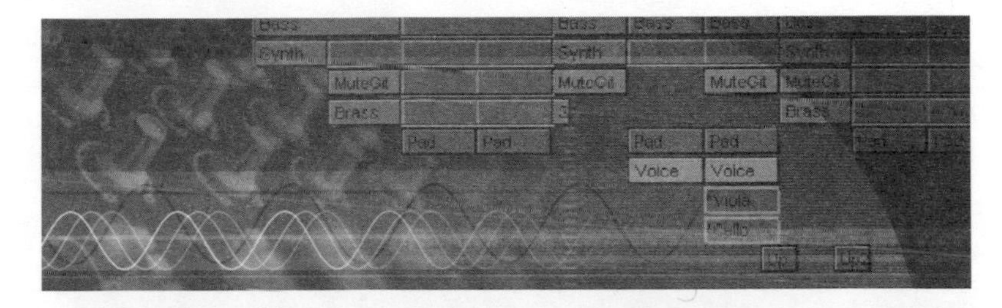

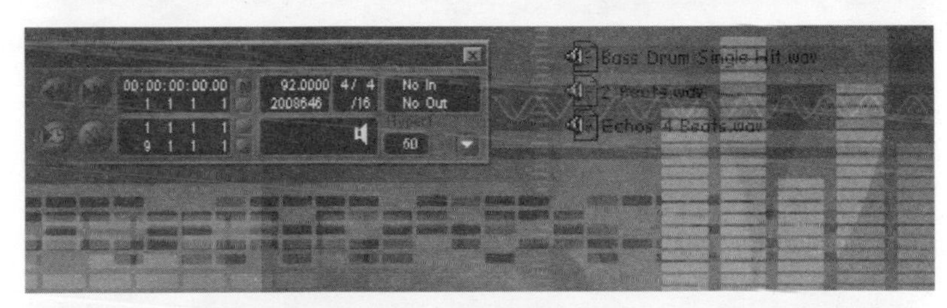

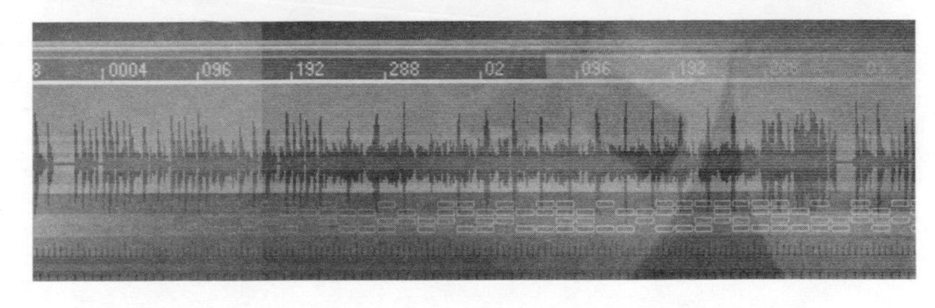

PC Publishing

PC Publishing
Export House
130 Vale Road
Tonbridge
Kent TN9 1SP
UK

Tel 01732 770893
Fax 01732 770268
email info@pc-publishing.co.uk
website http://www.pc-publishing.co.uk

First published 2000

ISBN 1 870775 68 6

British Library Cataloguing in Publication Data
A catalogue record for this book is available from the British Library

Printed in Great Britain by Martins the Printers Limited

Contents

Preface

Virtually every recording now made uses digital recording techniques. If it's on CD or DVD then at the very least, digital recording was used to create the final master, and in 99.9 percent of cases, you can bet that the whole album was recorded digitally.

Even though many of the larger studios still have monster reel-to-reel tape recorders, most now rely heavily upon digital recording. It's easier, it's faster, it's more flexible and it's better quality than tape recording.

But the really great thing about digital recording is that everyone with a PC can do it. You no longer have to spend five-figure sums on recording equipment in order to get professional results. Of course, as with all areas of technology, spending a little more on quality equipment will pay dividends, but a modern computer, a sound card and some software (which need not cost the earth) is all you need to get started.

This book has been written for several kinds of people. It's for anyone who wants to record sound on their computer, whether it's songs and music, special sound effects, voice-overs or even compiling audio CDs. It's for anyone who has a computer with a sound card and who wants to know how they can use it creatively. It's also for anyone who is interested in recording who may not have a computer and who wants to know what equipment they need and what they can do with it.

This *Quick Guide to Digital Audio Recording* is designed to give you the essential information you need to become familiar with all aspects of digital audio recording as quickly and as concisely as possible.

Dedication

For Monty,

...who broke all records...

With much love, still...

1

What is digital audio?

Digital audio is simply sound (audio, in other words) converted into a digital format.

There, that was easy, wasn't it?

This conversion takes place during recording and the data is stored on a computer's hard disk. The process is commonly referred to as direct-to-disk recording. Audio files can be saved in one of several formats (which we'll look at in Chapter 3), edited and processed in ways which could not be imagined when the only recording system was a tape recorder.

Why digital audio?

There are several Good Things about digital audio, particularly when you compare it with the alternative which is recording to tape. Here's a few comparisons between the two methods of recording.

Tape recording	Digital audio
Sound is stored on tape as magnetic signals	Sound is stored on hard disk as digital data
Copying a tape adds noise and produces an inferior copy	Copying digital data produces an exact copy of the original
Making a copy of a copy of a copy quickly destroys the quality	Copies of digital copies are exactly like the original
The inherent qualities of tape limit its audio quality	A good digital audio recording will be higher quality than a tape recording
You must wind the tape to access a section in middle or end of a piece	You can immediately jump to any point in a the digital recording
A part which appears in a piece more than once must be recorded each time it occurs	A part recorded once can be used any number of times anywhere in a recording
The number of tracks you can record is limited by the tape recorder you use	The number of digital audio tracks is limited by the power of your computer system
Each take uses a separate track. When you run out of tracks, some must be deleted	You can create as many takes as you wish, saving each one to disk
Editing is limited to punching in and out during recording and splicing the tape	It's easy to home in on the smallest part of a recording for editing
Effects must be added using outboard FX units	There are dozens of digital effects software which keeps the signal in the digital domain
The output from an effects unit must be recorded to another track or tape machine	Many digital audio effects run in real-time and the result can be saved as a new file, again, maintaining quality

Digital audio wins out on all counts – it's higher quality and more flexible.

Let's compare typical recording processes. Because tape is a linear medium you must start recording your song at the beginning of the tape and work through to the end. Not an unreasonable modus operandi you might think, but you can't, for example, record the chorus or the ending first. At least you could but you'd have to record the other sections on another tape and then copy all the parts to yet another tape, a process which is very fiddly and which reduces the audio quality.

With direct-to-disk recording, each part is stored as a file on disk. Using an audio sequencer, parts can be assembled and played back in any order you wish. The same part can be used several times which is ideal for constructing drum patterns and music lines from riffs and for making sure all the choruses are the same.

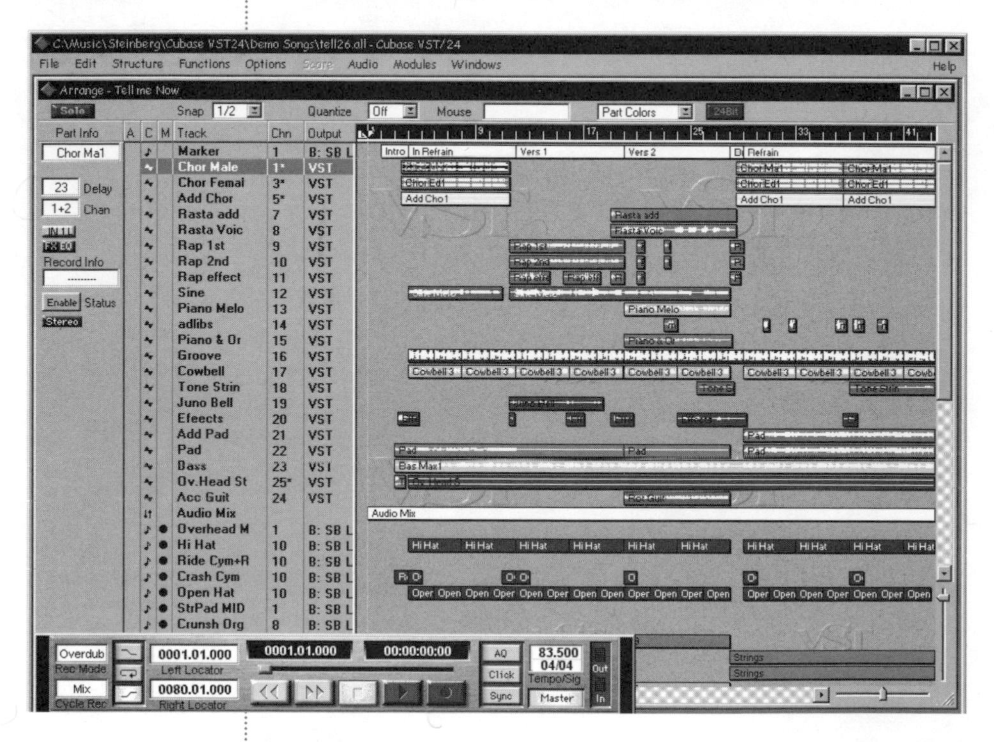

Figure 1.1: Each pattern represents a digital audio file on disk and the patterns can be placed anywhere in the arrangement.

Digital audio vs MIDI

Although digital audio and MIDI are both digital music formats, it's important to recognise the difference, so if you're new to computer-based music making here are a few words of explanation.

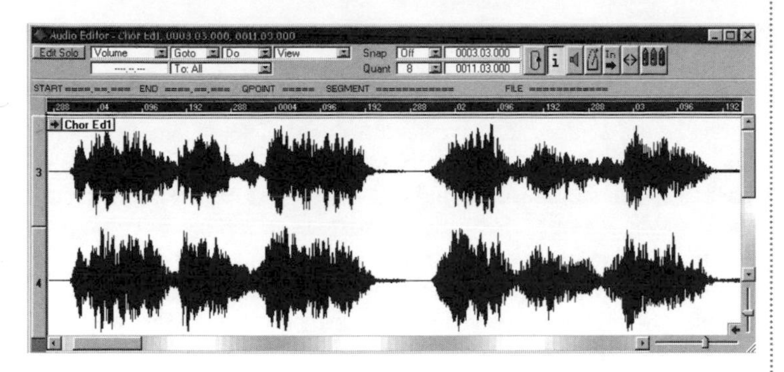

Figure 1.2: An audio recording contains a digital representation of the actual sound.

Digital audio as we've been discussing it involves the conversion of sound such as vocals or a sax into digital data. In other words, this data contains everything that was present in sound – the notes, the tone, the volume, everything.

MIDI stands for Music Instrument Digital Interface. It's actually a communications protocol designed to enable musical instruments to talk to each other. When you press a key on a MIDI-compatible keyboard it generates a series of messages. These include which note was pressed, how hard it was pressed and how long it was held down for. These messages can be sent to another keyboard (or recorded into a sequencer for playback later) and that keyboard would play back exactly the same note.

But what is not transmitted via MIDI is the 'sound'. If a piano was selected on keyboard 1 and strings on keyboard 2 then notes played on 1 would sounds as strings on keyboard 2. You can change

Figure 1.3: A MIDI recording consists of lists of music instructions.

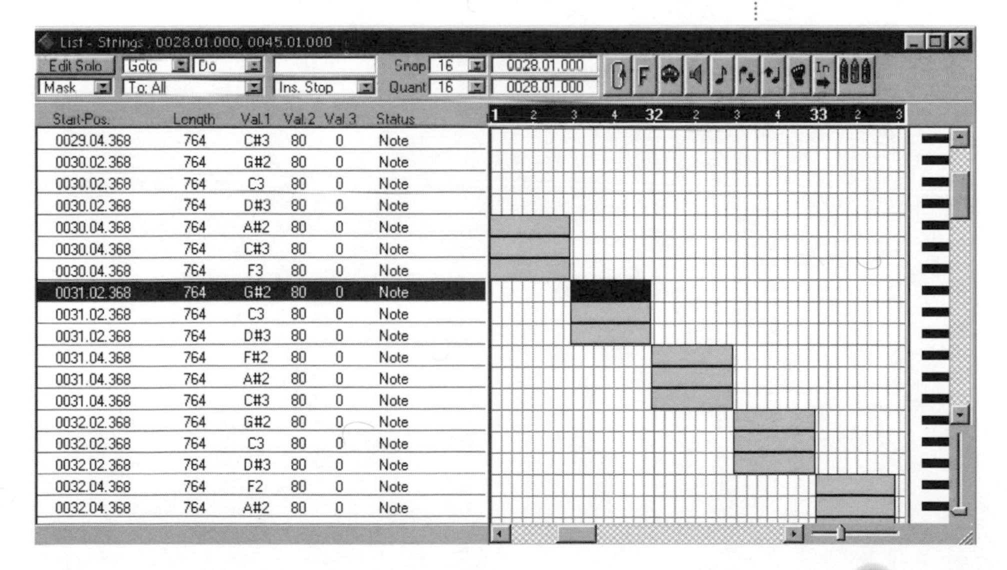

the selected sound via MIDI by sending Program Change messages but this only changes the preset on the receiving instrument. You cannot transmit the sound itself. Which makes sense. Let's say you were playing a very expensive keyboard with a set of superb sounds. It's unreasonable to expect that you could transmit these sounds to an El Cheapo keyboard to make it sound like the expensive one. Well, maybe it's not unrealistic to expect such a thing in this age of technological marvels but music technology can't do that yet!

So basically, MIDI messages consist of music instructions which specify the notes to play and how to play them. Digital audio contains the entire sound.

In the next few chapters we'll look at essential digital audio info and explain what features to examine when looking for computer recording equipment.

2

Sound basics

Sound is the raw material we work with when recording so it's useful to know a little bit about it. If you're new to this, don't worry – we'll keep the technicalities to a minimum but do read it through because it relates to the hardware and the digital audio functions we'll be discussing later.

Sound waves

So what is sound? Basically, it's a series of vibrations which are generated when an object is 'excited' by being hit, plucked, rubbed or blown into. Vibrations travel through the air and can be captured by a microphone to be recorded or enter our ears to play upon our eardrums which send messages to the brain which interprets the vibrations as 'sound'. Our ears and brain are actually incredibly clever as you'll come to realise. They can analyse nuances of sound which even the most sophisticated computer equipment cannot interpret. At least not yet.

Sound has three main attributes – amplitude (or volume), frequency (or pitch) and tone (or timbre). These three characteristics enable us to distinguish one sound from another. By displaying an audio recording in a waveform format – as all digital audio software does (see Figure 1.2 in the previous chapter) – you can discover information about all three characteristics.

Amplitude

This is an easy one. The greater the amplitude, the larger the sound wave and the louder the sound. Figure 2.1 shows a sine wave which produces a pure flute-like tone. Figure 2.2 looks the same but the waves are not so high. In other words their amplitude is less and these sine waves will be quieter than the others.

It's fairly easy to see how loud a sound is by checking the size or amplitude of the waveform against the scale in a wave editor. The examples here are taken from Steinberg's WaveLab, and the scale on

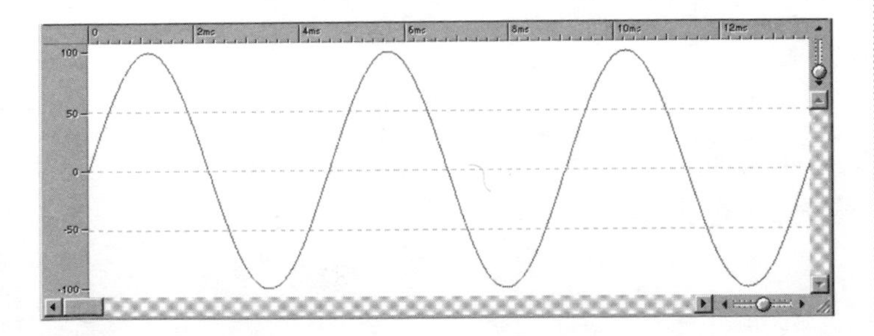

Figure 2.1: A simple, pure sine wave.

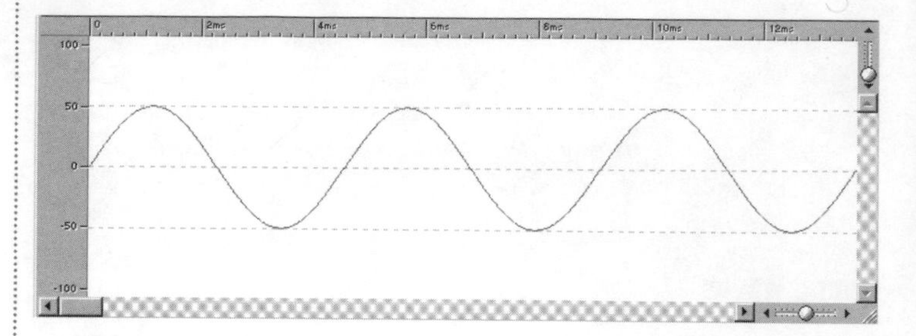

Figure 2.2: The same sine wave but at a lower volume.

the left runs from 0 to 100. You can see that the amplitude of the wave in Figure 2.2 is half that of the one in Figure 2.1 and so it will not be so loud.

Frequency

Frequency is also easy. The more waves there are in a given time period, the higher the frequency or pitch. Technically, this is measured in Hertz (abbreviated to Hz) which is the number of times per second each waveform cycle occurs. For reference, Middle C on a piano has a frequency of 261.63Hz.

In Figure 2.3 there are twice as many sine waves as in Figure 2.1. This means there are twice as many vibrations per second which we perceive as an increase in pitch.

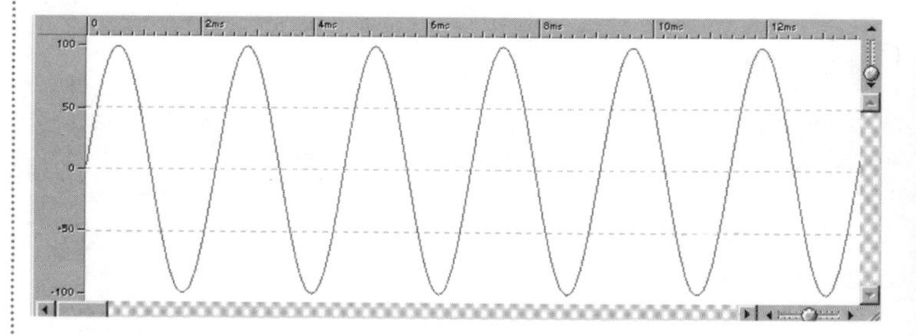

Figure 2.3: This sine wave has twice as many cycles per second as the one in Figure 2.1 and will sound an octave higher.

As with amplitude, it's easy to see the relative frequency of a waveform in an wave editor, providing the waveform is symmetrical. However, most natural sounds are not regular and it's by no means easy to hazard a guess at the frequency of the waveform in Figure 2.4. You can tell, however, that the waveform is only about half the level it could be and if we scroll thorough to the end of the file, Figure 2.5, you can see that peaks of the recording are pushing full volume.

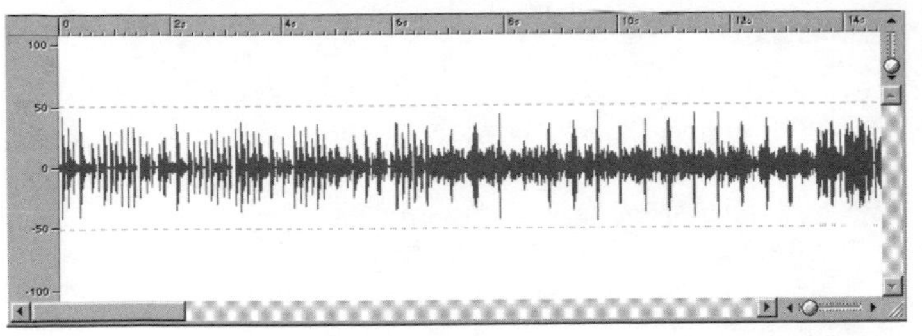

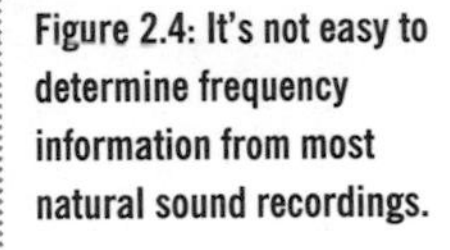

Figure 2.4: It's not easy to determine frequency information from most natural sound recordings.

Figure 2.5: Still not much frequency information but we can see that the amplitude of the peaks is greater.

Tone

Okay, this is a toughie. It's not easy to gather much information about the tone of a sound by looking at its waveform other than to tell if it's a simple or complex sound. Simple sounds have regular waveforms such as the sine wave we've been looking at, and there are square, triangular and sawtooth waveforms, too.

Most natural sounds – and synthesised sounds, too – are quite complex and are more likely to look like the waveforms in Figures 2.4 and 2.5. The complexity of a sound depends upon the number of additional waves or harmonics it contains. For example, a sine wave is simply a wave containing a single pitch known as the fundamental frequency. If you add another sine wave of a different pitch the tone will become more complex and the shape of the wave will change. The Square wave in Figure 2.6 is essentially a collection of sine waves containing odd numbered harmonics relative to the fundamental wave. You can't tell this by looking at the waveform.

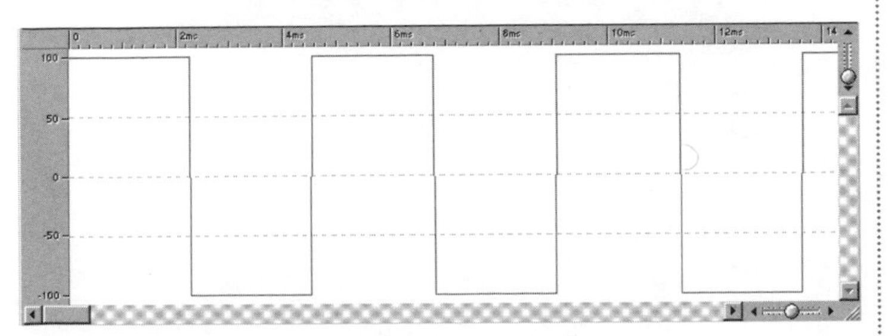

Figure 2.6: A square wave contains odd-numbered harmonics, not that you can tell by looking at it. For that you need FFT analysis.

FFT analysis

However, you can see it if you perform an FFT or Fast Fourier Transform analysis on it. This is simply a clever technique for analysing and displaying the frequencies in a sound. Several waveform editors have such a function built-in.

So take a look at Figure 2.7 which is an FFT of the square wave in Figure 2.6 and you can see the frequencies it contains. For comparison, Figure 2.8 contains the FFT of a pure sine wave and Figure 2.9 is the FFT of the waveform in Figure 2.5, which just goes to show how complex natural sound is and how many harmonics they contain.

In case you're starting to think the technicalities are entering the realms of scientific mumbo jumbo, stay with it because frequencies and harmonics play an essential role in the creation of a well-balanced sound as we'll see in Chapters 7 and 8.

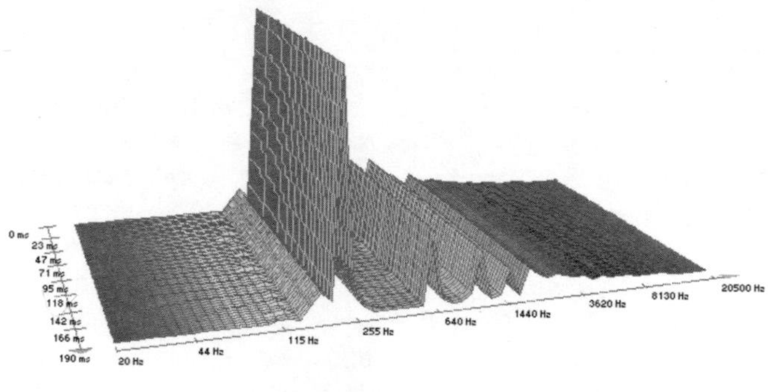

Figure 2.7: An FFT analysis of the square wave in Figure 2.6 shows the odd harmonics it contains.

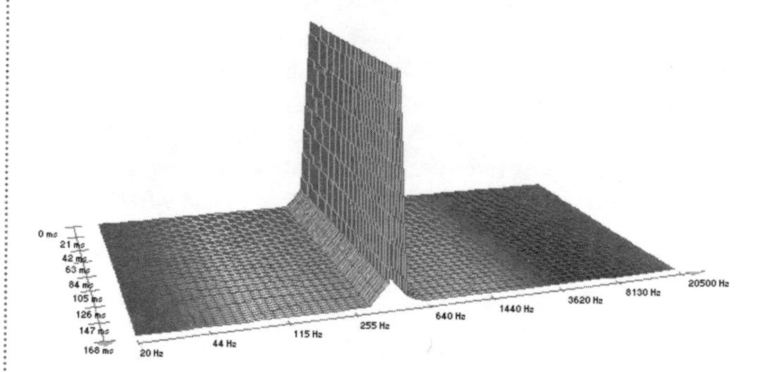

Figure 2.8: For comparison, the sine wave contains only one harmonic which is its fundamental frequency.

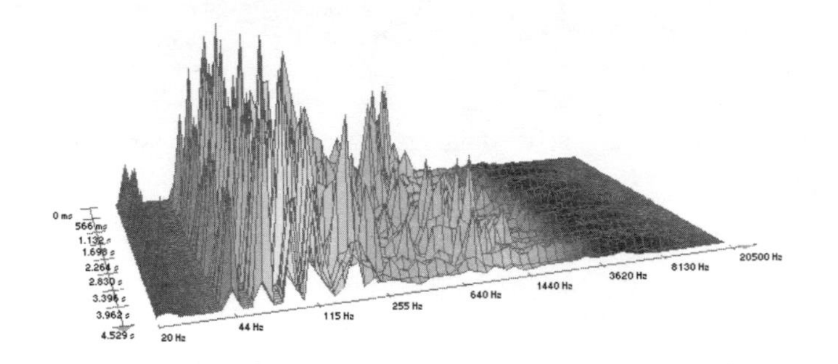

Figure 2.9: The FFT of a natural recording contains lots of frequencies and harmonics.

Decibels

How do we measure loudness? It's measured in decibels (usually abbreviated to dB) and if you're suffering from technology saturation this is probably good time to put on the coffee pot. Don't worry, this is the most techy chapter of the whole book.

The measurement of loudness is complicated slightly because we perceive loudness in a logarithmic way. Our perception of loudness is directly governed by the amplitude or intensity of the sound wave. In order for us to register a sound as being twice as loud as another its amplitude (intensity or sound pressure level) must actually be ten times greater.

That alone would be okay – we all did logs in school right? Right? But for a variety of historical and scientific reasons which you really don't want to be bored with – trust me on this – the decibel measuring system is not an absolute one but a relative one. Which means that you can't really say that a sound has a loudness of 6dB, for example. What you can say is that one sound is so-many dB louder relative to another.

Now before you throw the book down in disgust, there is a bright side. Not many people actually understand this (no, not even studio engineers!) so don't worry about it. The important thing to remember is that most volume-measuring equipment, including the recording meters on digital audio recording software, uses a decibel scale. An increase of 6dB is a doubling of the volume. An increase of another 6dB would double the volume again so 12dB is a four-fold increase in volume. 18dB is an eight-fold increase.

TIP

Here's the bottom line – if in doubt, just keep your eyes on the meters and your ears on the mix.

Dynamic range

Dynamic range is the difference between the loudest and quietest parts of a recording. And it's measured using our friend the decibel. Much modern music has a 0dB range. In other words it all plays at the same volume. Okay, kids, just a joke. Orchestral music often has a vast dynamic range, perhaps 90dB or more. It's all those *ppp*s and *fff*s that do it.

A good digital audio system ought to have a dynamic range of at least 90dB or more. There's more about dynamic range in the next chapter.

Signal-to-noise ratio

Signal-to-noise ratio is closely related to dynamic range. It's prevalent in audio equipment specifications so it's important to know what it means so you know what to look for in the specs.

Simply, it's a measurement of the ratio between the signal (the sound, the music or whatever you're recording) and the background noise of the system. It's often abbreviated to SNR or sometimes just S/N. Again, it's measured in dB.

SNR is related to dynamic range because the greater the dynamic range, the greater potential there is for a large SNR. And the higher the ratio the more 'sound' you can record with the system.

With a tape recorder, for example, there is always a high noise level because this is inherent in the tape medium. A cassette recorder might have a SNR of around 40dB. Switch in noise reduction and it might rise to 50dB. One of the advantages of digital recording is that it does not have this background noise, and even a modest digital audio system ought to have a SNR of around 90dB. There's more about this in Chapter 4. A good CD player might have a SNR of 93dB.

3

Digital audio basics

Now that we're on first name terms with our raw material – sound – we'll see what happens to it when we digitise it.

There are two digital audio parameters that crop up in every aspect of digital audio recording from the software to the hardware. These are the sample rate and the sample resolution, and on these hinge the overall quality of the digital audio.

Essentially, the sample rate determines how often the audio material is measured – or sampled. The sample resolution is the fineness of the measuring scale used. It's essential that you understand what these are and the part they play in determining the quality of your audio recordings.

Sample rates

First of all, we need to know how sound is converted into a digital format? Quite simply, we measure, or sample, the sound so-many times per second, and this is known as the sample rate. The more samples we take in a given time, the more accurate the digital representation of the sound will be. This is easily illustrated using a sine wave as an example.

The picture on the left shows a sine wave which has been sampled so-many times a second. It obviously looks like a sine wave but you can see that it has a few 'edges'. If we increase the sample rate so we take more samples each second, the digital representation of the wave becomes more accurate as you can see on the right.

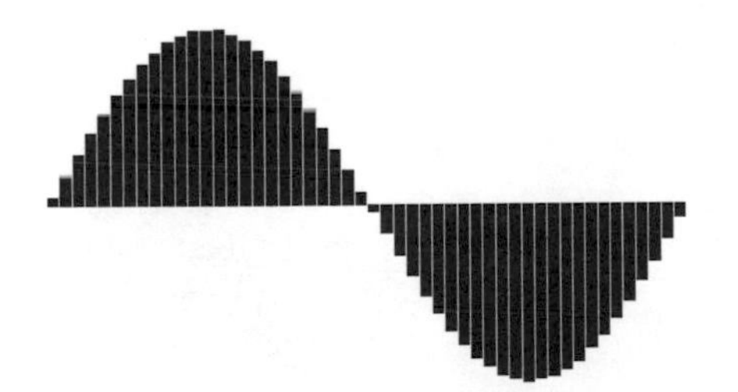

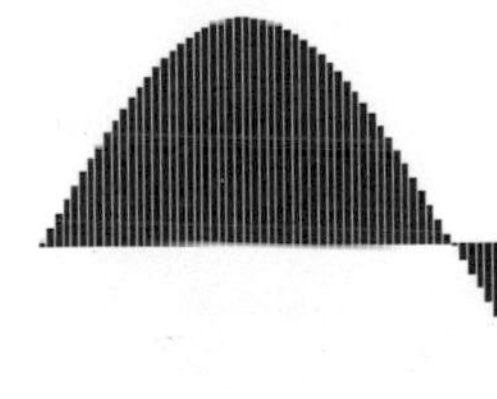

Figure 3.1 (left) shows a reasonable digital representation of a sine wave. However, by increasing the sample rate (right) the sine wave becomes even better defined.

Finally, Figure 3.2 shows a near-perfect digital representation of a sine wave which has been sampled at a very high sample rate. Contrast this with the waveform on the right which has a very low sample rate indeed. The sine wave shape here is only barely distinguishable.

So the best sample rate to use is the highest, right? Right! But we don't have to sample a zillion times per second; it's simply not necessary. Audio CDs use a sampling rate of 44.1kHz (that's 44,100 times per second) and that's generally considered good enough. You want to know why? Of course you do, so read on.

Figure 3.2: The left hand picture shows a well defined example which was recorded with a very high sample rate. Contrast this with the picture on the right which was sampled at a very low rate and which barely retains its sine wave shape.

Human hearing

Mathematician Harry Nyquist discovered that in order to sample a sound accurately it must be sampled at twice its frequency. Now, the range of human hearing runs from around 15Hz to 20kHz. Some people can hear sounds below and above these limits but that's about average. So, in order to sample the highest sounds we can hear – 20kHz – we need to use a sample rate of at least 40kHz. So 44.1kHz ought to be well enough to capture the full range of human hearing.

All modern audio recording software and hardware can sample at 44.1kHz. However, many systems support even higher sample rates. For example, DAT machines typically use 48kHz and it's not uncommon to see even modest digital audio systems supporting 96kHz. These higher rates allow an even broader range of frequencies to be captured, although you may need a good pair of speakers – and a good pair of ears – to be able to hear the difference between 44.1kHz and 48kHz.

Lower rates for samplers

Most systems offer lower sample rates, too, such as 22.05kHz and 11.025kHz. These will not produce good quality audio although if the audio you are sampling is in the lower frequency band it may not sound too bad. Some musicians deliberately record some sounds at lower sample rates in order to get a grunge or lo fi effect.

If you need to produce small audio files for a lo fi demo for sending over the Internet, do all the work at a higher rate and reduce the sample rate as the last step in the process. This will produce a higher quality file than doing all the work at the lower sample rate. There's more about this in Chapter 7.

Sample resolution

The sample rate determines how often we sample a sound. The sample resolution determines the measuring scale we use when taking a sample. The basic principle is that the larger the measuring scale (that is, the more numbers we can use to measure the sample), the more accurate the result.

Here's an example. Let's say you want to measure the length of your garage to see if a new car you're thinking of buying will fit inside. And let's say you're using one of these new fangled radar/sonic/laser beam all-electric digital tape measures, the sort of thing estate agents use to save them scrabbling about with a tape measure. And let's say that the digital readout is only calibrated to report measurements to the nearest foot (or 30cm if you're metric).

You're not going to get a very accurate picture of your garage, are you. Because the readout is digital, it can't report 'half-foot' sizes, for example. It will tell you that your garage is either 14ft or 15ft. If it was, in fact, 14½ft you wouldn't know because the measure doesn't do halves.

If, however, it measured to the nearest inch, you would get a much more accurate reading and although you may not know if your garage was actually 14ft 6ins or 14ft 7ins, it would probably be close enough for jazz, as they say.

We'll move on to sampling sound. If the measuring scale we use is coarse like the 1ft tape measure, we won't get a very accurate picture of the sound. A finer scale with more divisions will give us a much more accurate picture.

Sample resolution is measured in bits and the two most popular resolutions in current use are 16-bit and 24-bit. Briefly (and you can gloss over this part if you wish), a bit is a type of number used by computers. 16 bits can represent values ranging from 0 through to 65535. That's 65536 individual values (0 counts as a number, too). You can work out how many values a so-many-bit number can represent by using 'to the power of'

$2^{16} = 65536$

8 bits represents 256 (2^8) different values. When we measure a sound, each sample is given a number in the range afforded by the number of bits. If a sound must be described using only numbers up to 256 it's not going to be as accurate as one which can be described in 65536. There are no fractions in the digital system so 8-bits is like our 1ft measure and 16-bits is like the 1in measure.

What it all boils down to is that the more bits you use, the more accurate the digital representation of the sound will be. CDs use 16-bit recording which is the most common resolution used today. However, many systems also support 20-bit and 24-bit recording and several support 32-bit recording. We'll see why right now.

INFO

To understand exactly how sample resolution works, we really ought to take a quick excursion into the world of bits and bytes. But you've probably had enough technicalities for one chapter and it's not absolutely essential that you know what bits and bytes are in order to select a sample resolution so we'll skip the techy bits.

Dynamic range

The quest for ever-higher sample rates and resolutions is the search to capture every last nuance of natural sound. The number of bits used has a close relationship to the dynamic range of a recording.

As we saw in the last chapter, dynamic range is the difference between the quietest and loudest parts of a recording. Now imagine a system which has only, say, four different volume levels. If there was any noise in the system, the lowest volume it could possibly be would be 1/4 of the maximum volume. Also, any volume changes would be accompanied by a rather jarring change in level as it moved up and down the rather chunky volume steps.

With 8-bit recording we have 256 steps to play with and while that's obviously a whole lot better than four, it's not really good enough for our ears. It provides a dynamic range of 48dB which might have been okay in the golden age of the tape recorder, but not now. 16-bit resolution is much better and offers a dynamic range of 96dB. This is getting close to the dynamic range of real world sounds and human hearing which is around 140dB.

Crank up to 24 bits and you get a dynamic range of 144dB. Yes, that should let us capture thc full range of sonic subtleties out there. Imagine, though, a 32-bit recording system with a dynamic range of 192dB. No sound would be safe! So systems use more bits than 16 in order to capture a greater range of sound.

However, even if you're happy with 16-bit resolution, and most people currently are, there's another reason to consider using a higher one and that's to do with headroom.

Clipping, headroom and recording

Let's say you're merrily recording a sound using 16 bits and a peak comes along which warrants a value of, say 65600. 16 bits has only 65536 values so what happens? The peak is chopped down to size. Well, down to a value of 65536 anyway.This is called clipping and it most definitely is not a good thing. It distorts the recorded waveform which results in a distorted sound. Not nice.

The moral of the story is that you cannot and must not overdrive the levels during digital recording. When recording to tape, many engineers push the levels a little. Tape can handle this and creates a saturation effect not totally unlike compression (see Chapter 7 for more about effects) which makes the sound warmer.

But you can't do this with digital recording so you may need to leave a little headroom during recording just to make sure the peaks don't go off the scale and get clipped. So, it's not unusual to find you're working with an actual resolution of 14 or 15 bits giving a dynamic range of 84dB or 90dB rather than the potential maximum of 96dB. But that's still pretty okay.

INFO

By using a 24-bit resolution, you can afford to leave a few bits loose for headroom and still have a monstrous 120dB dynamic range.

The size of audio

So, after ploughing through all this you might be wondering why we don't simply record everything at 96kHz and 32-bit. One day we probably will but the hardware which can handle this is still relatively expensive, at least compared to systems which support 16-bit, 44.1kHz recording. You need a lot of processing power to handle that amount of data and more storage space to store it all.

So-called CD quality recordings (16-bit, 44.1kHz stereo audio) use around 10Mb of space per minute of recording. So let's say you're working on a 16-track, five-minute song; that could need around 400Mb of disk space. If you're putting together a 60-minute album that becomes 4.8Gb, not counting multiple takes and scratch files. You want more tracks? Multiply that figure accordingly.

Double the resolution up to 32-bits and you double the storage space. Increase the sample rate to 96kHz and you more than double the storage space again. So that same album could, theoretically, require over 20Gb of space. But heck, what's the big deal? 20+Gb drives are commonplace.

It's no big deal, but remember you will also need comparable amounts of processing power as you crank things up.

TIP

Here's a quick tip for equating bits to dynamic range. Multiply the number of bits by 6 to get the dynamic range. For example, 16-bit recording has a potential dynamic range of (16x6) 96dB.

Digital audio formats

On the PC, digital audio is usually saved in Windows' Wave format with a .WAV extension. This is the default format for all audio files and it's compatible with all audio software. On the Mac, the most popular format is AIFF (on the PC this has a .AIF extension) although some software also supports other formats such as SD II (Sound Designer II, named after Digidesign's eponymous audio editor).

Most audio software can load and save audio files in other formats which can be useful but unless you have a specific reason to work in another format, stick to Wave and AIFF. If the finished recording needs to be in a different format, convert it after completing the project.

MP3 files

If you're wondering about MP3 files, you'll find more about them in Chapter 9.

The bottom line

Today, most people probably do 'CD quality' recording using a sample rate of 44.1kHz and 16-bit resolution. This knocks the pants off tape-based systems and if you don't use anything less, your recordings should be good quality.

However, many pro systems are moving up to 24 bits and promoting 48kHz and even 96kHz sampling rates. These, obviously, require more computing power and you will also need a good audio system to appreciate the extra quality they provide.

Computer and system requirements

Now with some digital audio basics under your belt, let's look at the sort of equipment you need in order to do direct-to-disk recording. The three essential parts of a system are the computer, the hard disk and the sound card.

Most direct-to-disk recording systems are based around a computer, although there are also many stand-alone hardware systems which still record to an internal hard disk. The specifications of these are generally fixed although you may be able to upgrade certain areas, perhaps by adding another hard disk. They are designed for robust performance but generally lose well out to computer-based systems as far as features and flexibility go. They are, however, ideal if you prefer using hardware to a computer but we'll say no more about them here.

The question, 'which computer?', is a thorny one because computer technology advances on a weekly basis and software developers keeping upping the system requirements needed to run their software with every new release.

The best overall advice anyone can give you is to buy the biggest, fastest, meanest computer you can afford! That will stave off the ravages of obsolescence for at least a month and it should ensure that you'll be able to run the latest music software releases.

Minimum specifications

On the box of most software programs you'll find a 'minimum specification' of the computer system required to run it. Ignore this! They are invariably over-optimistic. Even if you could shoehorn the program into such a machine the chances are it wouldn't do much.

If you see a 'recommended specification', take this as an average spec. It ought to do the job but if you really want to see sparks fly you'll probably need something even better.

The fact is, most digital audio software, whether it does direct-to-disk recording, digital effects processing or runs a software synthesiser, can easily run even the most up-to-date computer into the ground. The capabilities of the software usually far outstrip the hardware's ability to deliver.

So it's usually a trade-off between how big a machine you can afford and the amount of processing you want the software to do. And it will ever be this way until they develop the 100GHz chip multi-processor computer. And even then you can bet some software developer will write an application which crawls along...

Having said all that, we'll throw in a few pointers which should help when you're speccing your machine.

PCs

The initial comment about buying the fastest you can afford applies. It's pointless specifying a minimum speed because chips get faster every day. Way back in 1965, electronics pioneer Gordon Moore predicted that the number of transistors on a chip would double every 18 months. This became known as Moore's Law and it has held up pretty well as the speed of computers has, indeed, continued to double approximately every 18 months.

Most software is developed on PCs containing Intel chips and although once upon a time one or two developers would not guarantee that their software would run on machines with a different processor, this is generally not the case now and other 'PC' chips ought to work fine, too.

However, chip sets are occasionally released with special go-faster features and if software has been written to take advantage of that then you'll obviously need the right chip. It will do no harm at all to ask the developer or distributor of the software about this before making a buying decision.

RAM

It's folly to even consider anything less than 128Mb RAM in a modern PC, particularly if digital audio processing is involved. Treat your machine and the software, give it room to breathe and stick in 256Mb. If you want to run a sequencer, a soft synth and some processing effects all at the same time, then 512Mb would not be too much.

Operating systems

Most folks use a version of Windows. While other Operating Systems such as BeOS have their attractions for multimedia use, there are far and away more music programs for Windows than all the other Operating Systems put together. And then some. You can always create a dual boot system and install BeOS, too, if you wish.

As of writing there are several versions of Windows. Many people are using Windows 98 (some are even using Windows 95) and this is currently, without doubt, the OS that most music programs are written for.

Windows Millennium Edition is based on Windows 98 and designed for Windows 98 users to upgrade to, so all Windows 98-compatible software ought to run under the Millennium Edition, too. But, as ever, do check before you buy.

Windows 2000 is based on Windows NT which some people will still be using. Win2000 is incredibly stable (as was/is NT) and if a program should crash, Windows will close it down without disturbing any other programs which may be running. Nice, that.

The problem with NT is that it was never well supported by sound card and music software developers, and often drivers were not available so you couldn't run your favourite software under it. The situation has been improving and we can only hope that the advent of Windows 2000 will improve it further but time will tell. Before buying either hardware, software (or PC and OS if you don't have them already), do check that there are drivers for the gear you want to use.

Macs

The options available when buying a Mac are somewhat less than when buying a PC. Only Apple makes Macs and when they introduce a new product range there may only be a handful of models in it.

But the same principles regarding speed apply when choosing a Mac. If Apple releases low-, mid- and high-end models, the high-end one is often stuffed with extras – maybe a larger hard disk, more RAM, a DVD RAM drive, perhaps a SCSI interface (SCSI used to come as standard on all Macs but was removed in the late 90s to cut costs) and it will invariably have a faster processor.

Check if you need these extras. Often the mid-range model offers the best value for money even if it means foregoing the delights of a faster chip, and you can easily add more RAM, another hard disk and even a SCSI interface if required.

Macs are usually intrinsically faster than PCs so you don't have to match processor speeds to get the same performance. Do regard 128Mb RAM as a minimum and why not make your Mac smile with 256Mb.

The iMac

It's worth devoting a paragraph or two to the iMac as it has been one of Apple's greatest success stories of recent years and is extremely well priced.

You can do digital audio on the iMac but it has several limitations you should be aware of. It has no expansion slots so you can't plug in a dedicated sound card (although a number of USB digital audio devices are available) or a SCSI interface. You can't open it to add another hard disk so must use a USB or FireWire hard disk. USB disks are not very fast and, therefore, not ideal for direct-to-disk recording. As of writing, FireWire has yet to prove itself.

When son of iMac Mk II or III appears some of these limitations may be removed. Meanwhile if you want to use an iMac, make sure you're aware of the limitations and add up the cost of the extras you'll need.

Hard disks

In direct-to-disk recording, digital audio data is saved to and read from the hard disk in real-time. It is therefore important that the disk is, literally, up to speed. If you buy a reasonably well-specified new computer system, the hard disk it comes with will probably work just fine. However, if you're thinking of upgrading your hard disk or adding another one, here's some information which will help.

The essential spec to check is the DTR (Data Transfer Rate) which is how quickly the drive can read or write a lump of data such as digital audio. Obviously, the faster the better but regard 11 or 12Mbps (Megabits per second) as a minimum rate which will still afford a useful degree of functionality.

IDE and friends

The 'standard' type of drive fitted in most PCs is colloquially known as IDE although when speaking of IDE drives many people also take in EIDE and UDMA drives (and ATA, too, although that is more correctly a type of interface). Although they work in slightly different ways they all connect to the computer in a similar way which is why they tend to get lumped into one group. (If there are any hard drive specialists out there, yes I know this is something of a simplification but it will do for the explanation in hand.)

Most modern drives are UDMA (Ultra DMA – Direct Memory Access) and offer transfer rates of 16.6Mbps, 33.3Mbps and 66.6Mbps. The computer's motherboard needs to support these rates, too – something else for you to check.

Since Apple stopped fitting SCSI to Macs as standard, the company have used IDE/ATA drives. The G4s have an ATA/66 drive which fair whizzes along.

For many users, these types of drive will do just fine but read on to see what the alternatives are.

SCSI

There are more versions of SCSI than spots on a Dalmatian. Transfer rates range from 5Mbps up to 160Mbps.

U2W (Ultra 2 Wide) SCSI with a transfer rate of 80Mbps is a popular and fast system, faster than the ATA/66 drive, but the more recent Ultra 3 supporting transfer rates up to 160Mbps is available for those who really need the speed.

The important thing to remember about SCSI is that you must match the SCSI hard drive to the SCSI card. It's no use plugging an Ultra 3 drive into a U2W card because you'll only get U2W performance.

SCSI devices are linked in a daisy-chain fashion and it's fairly easy to add another SCSI drive to your system, maybe up to 30 depending on the SCSI system in use.

SCSI can also handle several commands simultaneously so a system can transfer data from several SCSI drives at the same time. An IDE system can handle transfers from only one drive at a time. This won't be a major issue for most people unless you are using multiple hard disks for recording, in which case SCSI will win out.

USB

The Universal Serial Bus has been around for a few years but seemed to take off only when Apple removed all other ports from the Mac. It was USB or die.

The USB interface can be used to connect all manner of devices such as scanners, mice and keyboards, MIDI interfaces and, of course, hard drives. What's nice about USB is that up to 127 devices can be connected at once and they are hot-swappable which means you can plug and unplug them without powering down the system.

The USB transfer rate, however, is a rather sober 12Mbps although USB Version 2 promises a stunning potential of 480Mbps.

Currently then, USB hard drives are not a good option for digital audio. But they may be when USB 2 arrives.

FireWire

When Apple removed SCSI from the Mac, it added USB and FireWire (technically known as IEEE 1394). FireWire is (yet) another 'standard' which supports transfer rates up to 400Mbps (that's around 50 Megabytes per second which will help you fill up your hard drive in no time at all) and is on schedule to hit speeds of 800Mbps!

FireWire was designed to integrate computers with consumer electronics and it's already widely used in camcorders, allowing you to transfer your videos to hard disk. FireWire supports up to 63 devices and is also hot-swappable.

The data transfer speed is limited by the capabilities of the FireWire devices and FireWire drives are taking a while to appear. The FireWire route is certainly worth investigating but do check hard drive capabilities carefully.

HD maintenance essentials

There's one essential piece of housekeeping you must do and that's to defragment or optimise your hard drives regularly.

When files are saved to a hard disk, the system stores them one after the other. When you delete a file it leaves a gap which the system may try to fill the next time it saves a file. If the file is too large to fit the gap, the rest of it is saved on other parts of the disk (Figure 4.1).

The constant saving and deleting of files can quickly lead to single files being split up or fragmented in several sections across the hard disk. This severely reduces performance because the drive head has to jump around to retrieve a file rather than simply read the data sequentially. The solution is to defragment often.

Windows includes a defrag utility. Right-click on a hard drive icon, select properties then click on the Tools tab and there you'll find a Defragment Now button. Close all programs before running this and don't interrupt it until it's finished. Go and read *War and Peace* because it takes an absolute age.

INFO

There are several faster commercial utilities which include a defragger. These include Norton Utilities which is very handy to have around anyway to ensure your system is in good working order.

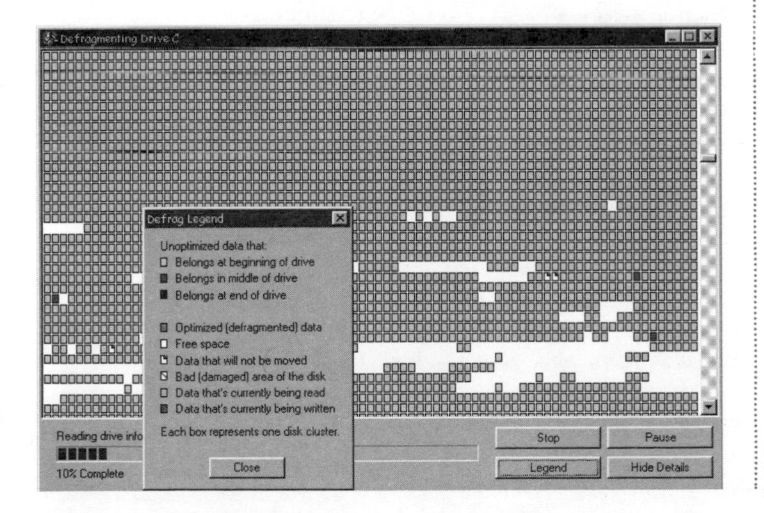

Figure 4.1: You should defragment your hard drives regularly.

INFO

The Mac OS currently does not include a defragger so you need to use a utility like Norton (yes, also available for the Mac). But use it you most definitely should.

Soundcards

Like computers, soundcards are under constant development and new models are released almost every week. It's important that you find a soundcard to suit your needs and pocket so we'll run through some of the features and specifications you need to look at.

Sample rate and resolution

Sample rates and resolutions were discussed in Chapter 3. It's important to find a card capable of the quality you require and possibly even higher if you think you may want to upgrade your system later, say to 24-bit recording.

For most people, 16-bit and 44.1kHz will be fine but you might like to consider whether 48kHz would be beneficial as it may simplify the process of digitally recording to DAT. (Although many DAT machines also support 44.1kHz, 48kHz will have the edge in quality.)

Frequency response

You want to capture the full range of human hearing (or pretty close to it) so the frequency response should run from 15Hz to 20kHz. Many quality cards have a range greater than this.

Dynamic range

We looked at this in Chapter 3. A card's dynamic range should be commensurate with its sample rate and resolution. A 16-bit card should have a dynamic range of at least 90dB.

Signal-to-noise ratio

Some cards quote a SN ratio rather than a dynamic range. It essentially describes how quiet a card is and it should be around 90dB.

You will see some SNR figures which have been 'A weighted'. The ear doesn't respond to all frequencies in the same way and SN ratios can be measured or weighted according to the way the ear responds to frequencies rather than the purely scientific unweighted measurement. This will inevitably produce a higher SNR figure than an unweighted measurement, all of which makes it difficult to compare cards if you're not comparing like with like. Some helpful manufacturers quote both weighted and unweighted figures.

Distortion

A little distortion in an electronic circuit is inevitable and you may see a THD (Total Harmonic Distortion) figure in some specs. We can usually detect distortion if it's between 0.5 and 1 percent of a sound's total harmonic content. Most THD figures will be below 0.005 percent.

Ins and outs

Of prime importance are the number and type of connections. If you intend to do little recording and mainly mix pre-recorded samples and sample loops you may need nothing more than a stereo input and a stereo output. If you want to record several instruments you will need more inputs. If you intend to mix down on the computer you may only need a pair of stereo outputs but if you want to run the signals through a mixer you may need six, eight or more outputs. Do you want pro XLR connections, are you happy with mini jacks or phonos, or do you want standard jack connections?

Do you need analogue or digital connections or both? With digital connections you can output the final recording to a DAT or to a digital mixer or effects unit. And, of course, you can record directly from a digital device which keeps the audio data in the digital domain. On the other hand, you can create a mix and save it to CD (see Chapter 8) so digital outputs may not be required.

TIP

Check how easy the connections are to access. Many trail around on leads behind the computer while other systems include a breakout box which is more convenient. Although if you're not constantly plugging and unplugging leads it may not matter so much.

On-board sounds

Do you want on-board sounds as well as digital recording facilities? The sounds on some cards are excellent particularly those based on wavetable synthesis. Other cards such as the Creamware Pulsar and Korg Oasys incorporate a dedicated synthesis system.

Soundcards for the Mac were traditionally audio only but now developers are producing Mac cards with built-in sounds. These include the Pulsar, Oasys and the Yamaha SW1000XG.

MIDI interface

If you want to combine audio and MIDI recording it may be convenient to buy a soundcard with a built-in MIDI interface. Most PC 'consumer' cards include a MIDI connection while some of the dedicated audio cards do not. Facilities on Mac cards vary but on the whole they tend not to combine audio and MIDI on one card.

Drivers

It is essential that suitable drivers are available for the card you buy when you buy it. Don't be fooled by 'coming real soon now' promises. Either wait until the drivers are available or buy another card.

TIP

The main issue here is OS-compatible drivers. If a card is released with drivers for Windows 98, for example, they may not work under Windows 2000. You might also want to check if specialist drivers you require are available such as ASIO (Steinberg drivers which can improve audio performance) or EASI (Emagic drivers).

5

Recording

There's more than one way to get audio data into your system and some, such as audio CD ripping and recording from a virtual instrument, are a direct result of digital audio technology. In this chapter we look at both these methods as well as 'traditional' recording.

Recording software has evolved into a handful of categories and while each has been designed with a particular purpose in mind, most share a core set of functions covering recording, editing and processing. So before we look at the recording process, we'll looks at the main types of audio software and the sort of features you might expect to find in them. There is also a list of some of the more popular programs in each category.

Multi-track audio sequencers

These are the computer equivalent of tape-based reel-to-reel multi-track recorders. Instead of recording to tape, you record to hard disk and recorded parts appear on tracks in the main arrange window. The really neat thing about this is that the parts on disk are 'referenced' by the parts on screen. This enables parts to be dragged to other positions and onto other tracks and the same part can be used several times in an arrangement even though it has only been recorded once.

Arranging and editing ought to be non-destructive. That is, changes you make to recordings are applied during playback so the original file is not altered (or else a new file implementing the changes is created).

The software should have a host of processing functions such as time-stretching and pitch-shifting (the ability to change the duration of a file without changing the pitch and vice versa), fades, normalisation (optimising the volume level), and EQ.

Check the number of tracks the software supports, that the sample rates and resolutions are compatible with your needs and your soundcard, and that it supports plug-ins.

There ought to be a mixer where the volume level and pan position of tracks can be set. Many mixers support automation which records adjustments you make to the controls and then recalls them during playback. Some systems also offer MIDI controlled mixing whereby controls can be adjusted via an external MIDI device such as a control panel or even the control wheels on a keyboard.

The final stage in music production is to mix the entire arrangement into a stereo file on disk for burning to CD. Some software includes CD burning facilities and an increasing number have an option to save files in MP3 format (see Chapter 9).

Software check

- Nuendo (PC)
- Samplitude (PC)
- Cool Edit Pro (PC)
- Pro Tools (PC and Mac)
- Deck II (Mac)
- Vegas Pro (PC)

INFO

There's more about plug-ins in Chapter 7.

Integrated MIDI and audio sequencers

Many programs started life as a MIDI sequencer and the developers added digital audio capabilities as the processing power of computers increased. MIDI and audio parts are shown in the same arrange window (Figure 5.1) making it very easy to work with both types of material.

Although many audio sequencers have a facility for playing MIDI files, if you want to combine MIDI and audio recording then an integrated program is definitely the way to go. The audio section of most such programs have the same facilities that you'll find in audio-only sequencers – often more – and include processing features, plug-in support, and audio editing.

Software check

Cubase VST (PC and Mac)

Logic Audio (PC and Mac)

Cakewalk (PC)

Digital Performer (Mac)

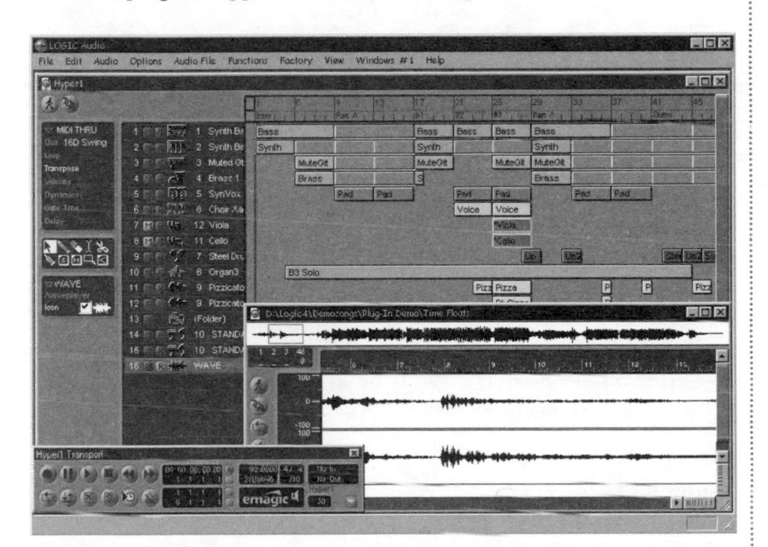

Figure 5.1: Emagic's Logic Audio combines MIDI and audio tracks on the some arrange pago.

Sample-based and loop-based sequencers

These are a relatively new kind of program, arriving in the late 90s and made possible by the increase in computer processing power. Some such as Acid work in a similar way to audio and MIDI sequencers by allowing you to arrange patterns on tracks to create a song. The difference is that they use audio samples and sample loops, so it can be rather like assembling a song rather than recording one.

However, the feature that made these programs so popular is their ability to change the tempo and pitch of the loops as they're added to a song to match the existing material. You can do this in other audio software, of course, using processing functions but it

Software check

Acid (PC)

Dance eJay (PC)

DJ2000 (PC)

3D Future Beat (PC)

Mixman Studio (PC and Mac)

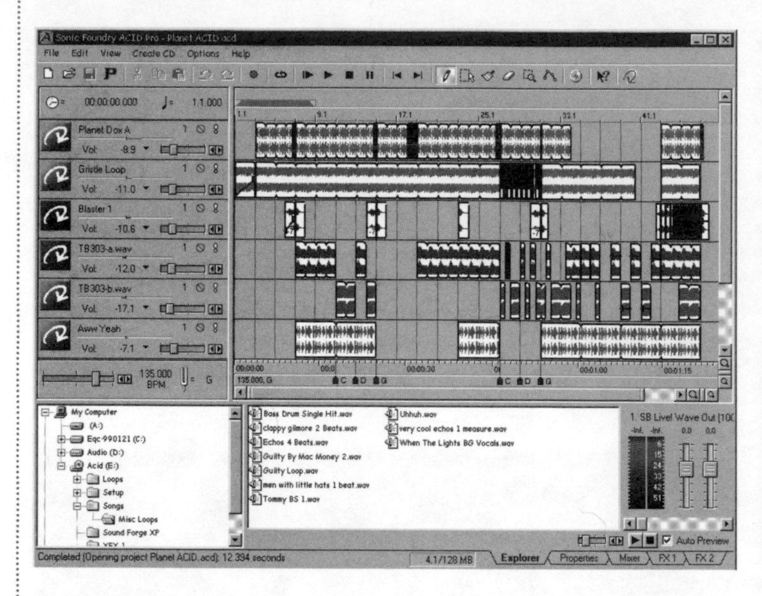

Figure 5.2: Sonic Foundry's Acid automatically adjusts the pitch and tempo of sample loops as you add them to a song.

can be long-winded and time-consuming and this type of software does it automatically.

Other programs work like a DJ mixing desk where you load a number of sample loops and trigger them in real-time or arrange them to play back in certain sequences. Some of these may seem a little lightweight. Many enable you to create (or assemble) music even if you have no music ability at all! However, they are great fun to use and most are quite inexpensive.

Audio editors

Audio editors are principally designed for recording and editing stereo recordings and usually have more edit features and fine-tuning abilities than audio sequencers. They can be used to home in on the smallest section of a recording, to tweak parts, to finalise a complete song or even an album before preparing a master, and, of course, for creating stereo recordings.

All major editors support plug-ins. Spark has a unique matrix system where effects can be linked and the sound processed through different combinations of effects. Some software can burn files to CD which is obviously convenient.

Audio editors are becoming increasingly sophisticated. WaveLab, for example includes a multi-track feature (it's almost a multi-track recorder) which is ideal for assembling audio clips and tracks into albums.

Software check

WaveLab (PC)

Sound Forge (PC)

Cool Edit 2000 (PC)

Peak (Mac)

Spark (Mac)

Not everyone will need an audio editor but if you need to do precision editing, batch processing, finalise material, or if you find yourself editing lots of stereo mixes, an editor may be a big help. There's more about editing in the next chapter.

As good as it gets

Recording is part art and part science. It's a vast topic so we'll concentrate here on a few essential principles.

There's an old saying, often heard when a recording is not going too well and the clock is ticking – 'we'll fix it in the mix'. This implies that a little EQ here and some compression there can turn a poor recording into a good one. It can't! It can probably *improve* a poor recording but it won't make it good. A track is not going to get any better than the raw material allows so it's worth spending time to make the recording the best you can in the first place.

Mic and line inputs

Use the correct input. Many soundcards have mic and line inputs. Without getting into the technicalities, microphones don't generate as much power or signal as line equipment such as synthesisers. Therefore many pieces of recording equipment, including mixers and soundcards, have both line and mic inputs. The mic input boosts the signal to bring it up to the level used by the system.

> **TIP**
>
> Using a mic with a line input will not produce a very strong signal and you risk adding noise to the recording. Plug a line signal into a mic input and you risk overloading the input and causing distortion.

Recording levels

The most crucial part of the recording process is getting the recording level right. Like analogue tape recording, the object is to get as much signal into the system as possible, without distortion or clipping (see Chapter 3 for more information about this). Don't try to record a part at a lower level because it won't feature prominently in the final song. The place to set the levels is at the mixing stage, not the recording stage.

To record at an optimum level, perform a dry run-through monitoring the input levels closely. If you can set a level and leave it there during the recording, fine. If you can't because the recording level varies so much (this is quite common with vocals), you might need to ride the faders during the recording process. Be aware that if the signal clips, it will most likely distort.

The meters in most software are very helpful and usually have a 0dB line above which you do not want the recording to go. They usually have a peak hold meter which stays lit indicating the highest level hit during the recording, just in case you blink!

Noise – and how to avoid it

The reason why you don't want to set the recording levels to, say, a safe half-way point is to maintain the dynamic range and achieve a good signal-to-noise ratio. Glad you read Chapters 2, 3 and 4 now, aren't you?

Apart from noise which may be introduced during recording, watch out for external sources of noise, too. These can obviously come from the recording environment when recording acoustic instruments. They can be minimised by using a cardioid or uni-directional microphone which only records sound coming from one direction.

TIP

If you can, place the computer in another room using extension cables for the monitor, keyboard and mouse.

Another potential noise problem is the computer itself. Most PCs have a fan mounted on the CPU chip itself plus one at the back of the case. All this processing generates a lot of heat. Even disk drives create noise, especially the faster ones which have a high rotation speed. You can minimise computer noise by keeping the cover on and perhaps covering it with a blanket or curtain – whatever you do DO NOT cover the ventilation slots.

Monitoring the recording

Monitoring, it must be said, can be a problem in some software. You want to see the levels in real-time and, if you're using a multi-track sequencer, you want to hear existing tracks as you record the new one so they are all synchronised.

With some software, the monitor signal runs through the system before being output so what you hear is actually delayed, a process known as latency. This is not good. If your system behaves like this, the best solution is to audibly monitor at source although you will still have to keep an eye on the recording level in the software.

Latency can be improved by well-written drivers, and some soundcards and their drivers have a very low latency indeed. Also, see if ASIO 2 drivers are available for your soundcard. These add a feature called Direct Monitoring which essentially routes the signal directly to the output socket as soon as it hits the input. Voila – no latency! But check that both the software and hardware support this.

Monitoring connections

As monitoring is such an essential aspect of recording, let's look at a couple of examples. First we'll see how to connect a system with poor latency by monitoring at source. The exact connections will vary according to what equipment you have but the principles are the same.

First of all, you want to hear what has been recorded so the soundcard's output must be connected to some speakers. If you want to record an acoustic guitar, for example, monitoring could be as simple as running the soundcard's output into a set of headphones instead and simply listening to the guitar as you play it into a microphone. Yes, this is the cheap and cheerful approach but it works. You can record other acoustic instruments and vocals in this way, too.

TIP

You should use enclosed headphones (ones which completely cover the ear) so the output does not spill into the microphone during recording. You'll find you don't need a loud or particularly hi fidelity monitor signal to be able to play along with it

Monitoring with a mixer

If you plan to record a lot of acoustic instruments each with their own output, a mixer can simplify the process of connecting them to the soundcard. If all instruments are being recorded via a microphone then more sophisticated set-ups probably aren't required ... other than for a small amount of convenience or unless you use several microphones.

If the soundcard has only one audio input you can connect several instruments to the mixer and route them one at a time to the input for recording. This can be done simply by muting unused channels. You might be thinking that you could also record several sources at the same time by combining them in the mixer. Although this may seem tempting, it's far better to record each instrument on its own track as this gives you far more control over the song during the arranging and mixing phases.

To monitor at source via a mixer, you need to mute or turn down the output to the speakers as before, and listen to the source's output through the mixer via headphones. Some mixers have a headphone monitoring facility so you simply plug into that.

If the mixer has an Aux (short for auxiliary) send (techy mixer term for output) you can use that. It taps into the mixer's audio signal to provide another output and, in fact, its most common use is precisely to send a monitor signal to a performer via headphones.

If your soundcard has several audio inputs they could be wired, more or less permanently, to the mixer outputs. This would require a mixer with at least as many outputs as instruments. You could not do this, for example, with a keyboard mixer designed to mix several signals into one stereo output. If you wanted to connect four instruments and your soundcard had four inputs you would need a mixer with four outputs and so on. Do bear in mind any requirements you may have for stereo recording. A synthesiser, for example, will almost surely have a stereo output. Vocals, and a bass guitar, on the other hand, don't need to be recorded in stereo and can simply be positioned where required in the final stereo mix.

Alternatively, the outputs from several audio sources could be connected directly to the soundcard inputs but you'd then need to monitor them as described earlier.

Pre-fade and post-fade

Many mixers have two Aux sends labelled pre- and post-fade. These simply refer to the Aux's position in regard to the volume fader. A pre-fade Aux takes its output before the fader so the fader has no effect on the Aux volume level which is usually adjusted with an Aux level control. This lets you set the volume of the monitor signal which does not change even if you adjust the fader. This is the one to use for monitoring.

Post-fade outputs are normally used to send a signal to an external effects unit. In most cases we want the amount of signal being processed to vary according to its volume level. Using reverb as an example, the amount of reverb applied to a signal should vary with the level of the signal otherwise it will sound off-balance and unnatural.

Do I need a mixer?

Whether or not you need a mixer depends on what you're recording, how you're mixing your material, whether you're using any outboard effects and how you're listening to the result. In practice, many smaller computer-based recording studios may not need a mixer. If you record one acoustic sound at a time, if you use pre-recorded samples, and if you use the computer to mix down the final recording into stereo directly to hard disk you may not need a mixer.

Oddly enough, if you use MIDI and have several MIDI synthesisers or sound modules, you will almost certainly need a mixer to bring all the signals together, even if it's just to listen to their combined output during playback.

TIP

When a song has been completed, some users may be tempted to feed the combined MIDI parts into the sequencer and record them as one track. It is far better, however, to record each one on its own track. As mentioned earlier this gives you far more flexibility when it comes to arranging and mixing.

DI – direct injection

The subject of DI or direct injection may crop up as you explore the world of mixers and recording so we'll look at that now. You can usually plug a synth, sampler or drum machine directly into the line input of a soundcard, but electric guitars and basses may not work so well. DI is usually used to connect a guitar to the mic input using a device known as a DI box to match the levels.

This works best when the signal is clean. If you have a killer sound created by playing a guitar through a combo amp, the best way to record it is via a mic placed in front the speaker. There's more about recording guitars a little later.

Mics

Like many aspects of recording, the art of microphone selection and placement is as much an art as a science, and more than one recording engineer has made a name by knowing the best ones to use in a given situation   or even when to break the 'rules' to create a special sound. There are several different types of microphone. The most common ones are dynamic and capacitor mics and we'll concentrate on those here.

Dynamic mics use a diaphragm attached to a coil to convert sound vibrations into an electrical current, a little like (if you remember your school physics) moving a magnet inside a coil of wire generates electricity. They are sturdy, require no external power supply and are relatively inexpensive. However, they are not so good at capturing high frequencies and while they are fine with loud, up-front sounds, anything a little pianissimo may not record very well.

Capacitor (also known as condenser) mics have a much thinner diaphragm whose movement produces variations in an electric current. They are much more sensitive than dynamic mics handling higher frequencies very well and they are suitable for both loud and quiet sounds. However, they do need a source of power (this often comes from the phantom power supply built into many mixing desks). They are not as sturdy as dynamic mics and they are generally more expensive.

There are also mics known as back-electret (yes, a development of the electret mic) which is a capacitor mic variant. They are more sensitive than dynamic mics and respond better to higher frequencies yet don't cost much more.

Microphone response

Microphone response is another consideration. In most cases, a unidirectional mic will be the best for the small studio. They pick up signals from only one direction which helps cut out background noise. They are commonly referred to as cardioid (which means heart) because the response pattern looks a little like a heart.

A hypercardioid mic has a narrow pick range to the front but is also more sensitive to sounds directly behind. There is also a figure-of-eight pattern which is sensitive to sounds at the front and back but not the sides. Finally, of course, there is the omnidirectional mic which picks up sounds from a full 360 degrees,

If you are not sure which type of microphone to get, most home or small studios should find a cardioid capacitor mic suitable for most uses. If you don't need to record quiet or distant sounds then you could look at a dynamic mic although a back-electret will be better. Generally, a capacitor mic will be more versatile.

Top – dynamic mic
Middle – Capacitor mic
Bottom – Mic responses

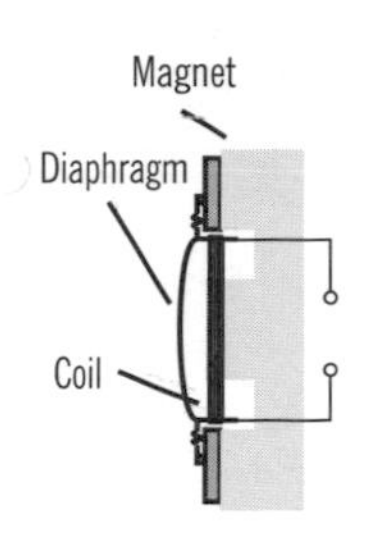

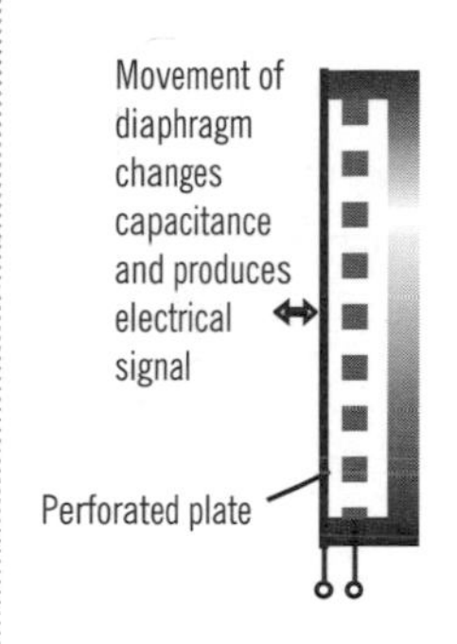

Recording techniques

Being able to make a good recording of an instrument is often the mark of a good engineer and while there's no substitute for a little experience, we offer a few tips and general rules which will put you on the right track.

Complete books have been written about mic placement for a whole range of instruments. The important thing to remember is that the environment plays a part in determining the overall 'sound' of an acoustic instrument. Bunging a mic in the end of a clarinet will not produce as authentic a sound as placing it a foot or two away. However, you generally do not want to absorb too much of the room by placing the mic too far away because that will colour the recording. You can add ambience later by applying reverb.

Here are a few simple tips for recording a range of sounds. In most cases we'll assume you are using a cardioid capacitor or electret mic.

Recording vocals

For most listeners, the vocals are the most important part of a song (although backing musicians know better!) so it's worth taking extra care to get them right.

Use a cardioid mic about 8 – 10 inches from the singer. You may find you need to use a pop shield to reduce plosive sounds such as B and P. (Many users make their own by stretching a pair of tights around a 6-inch frame made from a wire coat-hanger. Not as elegant as a professional shield but much cheaper.)

The recording environment should usually be deadened which can be done by draping curtains over reflective walls. Again, effects and ambience can be added afterwards. The singer should stand to allow their diaphragm to move freely. If you want an intimate vocal effect, they can move closer to the mic but be aware that this can increase the bass. Some mics have a bass roll switch, otherwise use the EQ in your software to reduce the frequencies around 80Hz.

INFO

There's more about EQ in Chapter 7

Recording acoustic guitars

The main thing to remember here is not to point the mic at the sound hole as the sound will be boomy. Point the mic at the bridge or at the top of the body where it joins the fretboard. Unless it's featuring as a solo instrument it's not necessary to record it in stereo. You can add a dash of pseudo stereo later (see Chapter 7).

Recording electric guitars

There are lots of options here. One is to use a DI box as mentioned earlier. However, if you want to use an effect such as overdrive or distortion, play the guitar through a combo and record with a microphone. Here you can use a dynamic mic and put it close to the speaker although it's worth experimenting with different positions. A capacitor mic further away will capture the ambience of the speaker. A close-miced amp is most often used for rock material. There are several plug-in effects which can be used to add overdrive and distortion effects (see Chapter 7).

Recording bass guitars

Many musicians DI a bass but some swear that this does not capture the full sonic thump of the original. In which case you can mic it in a similar way to an electric guitar.

Recording wind and brass instruments

Most orchestral instruments of this type can be recorded quite successfully by placing a mic anything from one to two feet in front of it (but do experiment). Don't point the mic directly at the bell (or the bit the sound comes out of as they say in Blyth).

Recording drums

This is a big subject and there are as many ways to mic a drum set as there are engineers. Pro studios tend to mic every drum but that's not always practicable for the smaller studio. A popular alternative is to use a couple of mics either above the kit or in front of it. The sound you get will depend upon their position and the ambience of the room but try a few feet above or in front and experiment from there.

If recording live drums is too difficult or simply not practicable, don't be afraid to use drum samples or sample loops or to program the drum track via MIDI. If you can find samples that you like and which fit the music, it saves a lot of hassle – although, of course, this isn't quite truly original material... MIDI drum tracks can be very effective, especially using some of the sample-based drum software which we look at any minute now.

TIPS

You can find lots more recording tips in the books, *Tips for Recording Musicians* and *Recording the Guitar* available from the same publisher which brings you this fine book.

Virtual instruments

It's but one short step from software which processes audio to software which generates it, and so the soft synth was born. Soft synths offer all the facilities of hardware synths – less the physical knobs, of course – with more flexibility and versatility, and at a fraction of the price. There are also soft samplers which let you load,

Software check

Model E
PPG Wave 2.V
Pro-Five
ReBirth
Reaktor
Dynamo
GigaSampler

edit and manipulate samples much the way hardware samplers do – but with all the benefits of running in software.

Originally, soft synths were stand-alone programs and, indeed, many still are. However, recent developments have gone even further and soft synths can now be 'plugged in' to sequencer software, just like digital effects. This has the great benefit of integrating the synth more fully into the recording environment making it easier to record, process and arrange the synth parts.

The integration has been greatly helped by the development of ReWire by Steinberg. This is a software link which routes the audio output of a soft synth to the host software's mixer. In the case of Cubase VST, the synth's output appears in the mixer and you can apply effects to it just as you can to any audio track. ReWire needs to be supported both by the synth and the host program. VST and Emagic's Logic Audio were the first two pieces of software to support it and no doubt others will, too.

INFO

There's more about plug-ins in Chapter 7 and more about ReWire in Chapter 8

The current standard for plug-in instruments is VST Virtual Instruments, originally developed for Cubase VST but also being supported by other developers. Emagic also has a format of its own for use within Logic Audio. There are several dedicated VST Virtual Instruments, with more appearing every month, and many soft synth developers are creating special VST Instrument versions of their programs, too.

Software check

Fruity Loops
ReBirth
LM•4
DR-005
Voodoo

Virtual drum machines

And it's no distance at all from a virtual instrument or sampler to a virtual drum machine. These tend to work like a sampler but with dedicated drum samples. Most allow you to load other samples so you can create your own drum kits, and there's nothing to stop you using other sounds, too. While some, such as the LM•4 and DR-005, are virtual instruments, others such as ReBirth and Fruity Loops are stand-alone programs.

Recording virtual instruments

Virtual instrument plug-ins all use MIDI data to generate their music lines. When plugged in to a MIDI or MIDI/audio sequencer, all you do is program a MIDI track and route it to the instrument. Here's how it works in VST.

First of all, access the Audio>VST Instruments menu which opens the VST Instruments module rack. Select a virtual instrument from the rack menu and then this will appear as an output option in the Arrange page in the MIDI tracks' Output columns. The main thing to remember is that you must open an instrument first before it appears in the Output column.

You can now play and record a MIDI part as if you were using a soundcard or external MIDI module and it will play through the virtual instrument. You do need to be aware of the latency situation though (for more about latency see the Monitoring section earlier in this chapter).

Recording stand-alone software synths

This can either be easy or less-easy... The more enlightened pieces of stand-alone software such as Reaktor and SynC Modular (a modular software synth freely available on the Internet) install a MIDI driver which enables them to be driven directly from a sequencer running on the same computer. Once installed, you'll find that outputs for these pieces of software appear in the MIDI output section of a sequencer. In the case of Cubase they are in the tracks' Output columns in the Arrange page. In Cakewalk they are accessed from the Options>MIDI Devices menu.

A complete description how these work is beyond the scope of this book but the main thing to remember is to *read the manual* because installation is just a little different to what you may be used to. However, if you follow the instructions, installation and operation is not difficult.

Using Hubi's MIDI Loopback Device as an example, it installs up to four extra 'MIDI ports' labelled LB1 to LB4. These show up in the software's MIDI port list (VST's Output menu, for example). In use, you assign the sequencer's MIDI track output to, say, LB1 and assign the soft synth's MIDI input to LB1. And then the MIDI signals pass from the sequencer to the synth.

Things work slightly differently on the Apple Mac where the most common form of MIDI data exchange is achieved via OMS, which is Opcode's Open Music System. This is a de facto standard (although there are other systems such as Mark of the Unicorn's FreeMIDI) and OMS comes with many pieces of music software and hardware and is freely available from the Internet. It essentially works in a similar way to Hubi's but setting up is rather more involved. Again, you must read the instructions carefully and take your time setting it up otherwise it will end in tears.

TIP

If the software doesn't come with its own driver you need to install a halfway house which links to both pieces of software. There are several options although two are in most common use – MIDI Yoke and Hubi's MIDI Loopback Device. They both work in similar ways although of the two, Hubi's seems to be the most popular.

Audio ripping

Yet another way to 'record' or input music into a program is to copy it from an audio CD, a process colourfully known as audio ripping. A CD ROM drive is now fitted as standard in all computers and most can be used to successfully copy audio from the CD to your hard disk using suitable software. This is particularly useful if you use audio

INFO

There's more about burning audio CDs Chapter 8

TIP

Transferring audio direct from CD to hard disk. rather than recording it from an analogue audio output. helps preserve the audio quality because it does not undergo the digital-to-analogue-to-digital conversion process.

sample CDs, although many sample CDs, sensibly, are now available in a digital audio format. Of course, audio extraction is also useful for creating your own CD compilation albums.

There are stand-alone audio rippers but some audio editing software such as Cool Edit 2000 also include an audio extraction function. Many pieces of Mac audio software can also rip audio CDs. QuickTime has built-in facilities for doing this, so it's fairly easy for a programmer to tap into this and add it to a program. Also, virtually every piece of software which can burn CDs has an audio extraction feature.

A couple of caveats. Although *most* modern CD drives can extract audio, some do it better than others. SCSI drives are generally better than ATA (IDE) drives.

Getting rid of the jitters

Some drives which do extract audio may not make a very good job of it and the resulting audio may contain crackles or distorted sound. This may be partly due to the drive and partly to the audio extraction software.

The reason jitter occurs is a little technical but it's to do with the way the data is stored on the CD and the way the drive has to read it and then write it to the hard disk (not going too fast here are we?) In essence, the drive has to pause after reading so the data can be written to the hard disk, and when it starts reading again it may not start from the exact place it left off which can result in uneven data transfer.

Some drives, however, compensate for this and the Plextor range of drives are highly regarded for their audio extraction capabilities. Good extraction software can also compensate but occasionally you may come across a drive which just doesn't the job well at all. Not much you can do about it other than get another drive...

Arranging

Now that the audio is inside the sequencer, let's run through a typical arranging session. Most multi-track sequencers work in a similar way by showing recordings as 'parts' or 'sections' on a series of tracks. As mentioned earlier, these actually reference the audio data on the hard disk and the parts can be moved, copied and processed in the sequencer very easily.

Using Cubase VST as an example, you can see in Figure 5.3 that most of the tracks have been constructed from several parts. In fact, many, such as the drum, ambient and bass tracks use just one part that has been copied to the track several times. This is a particularly

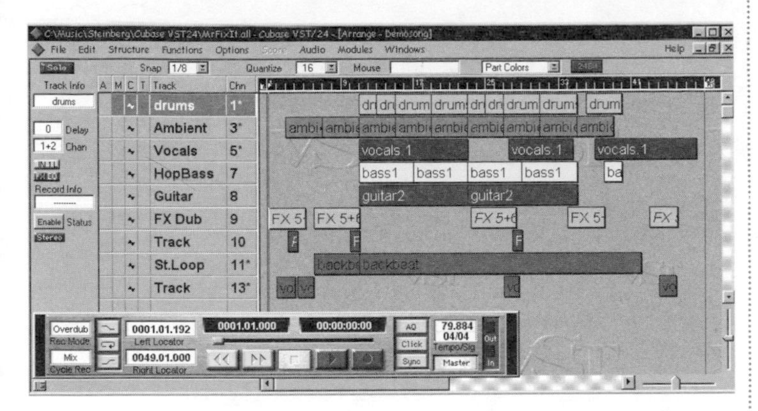

Figure 5.3: The arrange window in Cubase VST showing how tracks can be built up from individual parts.

useful way of building up a drum track from a drum loop which might be two or four bars long. Even vocal recordings of, say, a chorus can be copied in this way. That's not to say that this is the only way or even the best way to create a recording. If a vocalist sings an entire song right through from the beginning to end it will have more spontaneity and variety than if you use the same chorus recording more than once.

However, this is a very useful technique for instrument parts although again, they will benefit from a little variety. For example, you wouldn't use the same drum loop for an entire song. Likewise, don't use it even for an entire section; break it up by adding an extra hit or drum beat here and there, and do use small drum breaks in the transition between sections, say from verse to chorus.

Aliases and ghost parts

We have talked about copying parts, but there is another way to 'copy' a part which, in many situations, is a better method to use. That is to create an alias or ghost part – the terminology varies from one program to another. A ghost part is a copy of an existing part but, if you alter the original part, the ghost part changes, too.

This is most commonly used with MIDI parts. Let's say you've recorded a bass riff which you copy to several places throughout a song, and then let's say that you decide to change it; it could be something as small as a single note. You'd either have to physically change every copy or else delete the original copies and copy the new part to all the correct positions. With a ghost part, all you do is edit the original and all the ghost parts change, too.

This works with audio parts too, although the scope for editing audio is probably not as great as for editing MIDI parts. However, it's a very useful technique to use if you think you may want to tweak a part here and there.

Editing

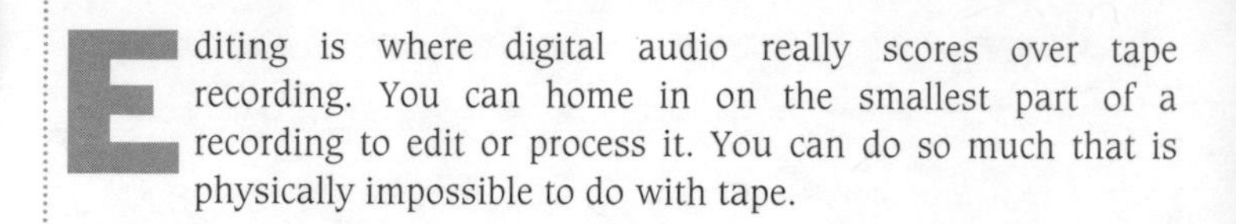

Editing is where digital audio really scores over tape recording. You can home in on the smallest part of a recording to edit or process it. You can do so much that is physically impossible to do with tape.

Non-destructive editing

Once a digital audio part has been recorded you can run it through all sorts of hoops without changing the original part. Most software does this automatically by applying changes on the fly during playback only, but at the very least you can make a perfect copy of it and perform your experiments on that.

A common requirement is to want to use different parts of a recording in different places in the arrangement. This is easily done by 'cutting' a part into sections and placing each section where it is required. The cutting doesn't touch the original recording at all. Instead the software simply uses the 'cuts' to refer to that section in the recording on disk and to play it when required. Copying can be done in the same way – by simply referencing the original file several times. Other edits such as creating fades or inserting silence can also be performed non-destructively.

All these functions are usually performed automatically. The user goes through the traditional cutting and editing processes and the software shuffles its reference points around accordingly. However, a lot of software also has a destructive edit function so do check that an edit will not permanently affect a file if you don't want it to.

INFO

Virtually all digital audio software has edit facilities to some degree although not all can get down to sample level. If you need such fine control over a recording, look at the audio editors mentioned in the previous chapter

Editing audio in a sequencer

When working with loops you may often want to change the length of a sample by a small amount to make sure it loops in time. For example, if you have a two-bar drum loop but only want to loop the first bar, you need to cut the sample at the precise point to make the audio exactly one bar long. If it is not, it won't sound right or it may run out of time the longer it is played (although there is a way to avoid this as we see shortly).

Trimming a sample is easily done in an audio editor where the start and end of a loop can be cut with great precision. However, you may also be able to perform similar functions in a sequencer. Cubase VST, for example, has a built in audio editor and while it is not designed for the precision editing offered by WaveLab or Sound Forge, it can be used to cut audio events and could, therefore be used to cut a two-bar sample in half.

However, there is a better way and, in keeping with the non-destructive editing ethos, that's simply to change the points at which the sample starts and finishes playing. Just as a part on a sequencer track references an audio file on disk, so we can tell the program exactly where inside the file to start and stop playing.

In Cubase, trimming a sample is easily done by dragging the handle at the end of an audio event as shown in Figure 6.1. This does not change the event in any way but simply determines which part of it plays.

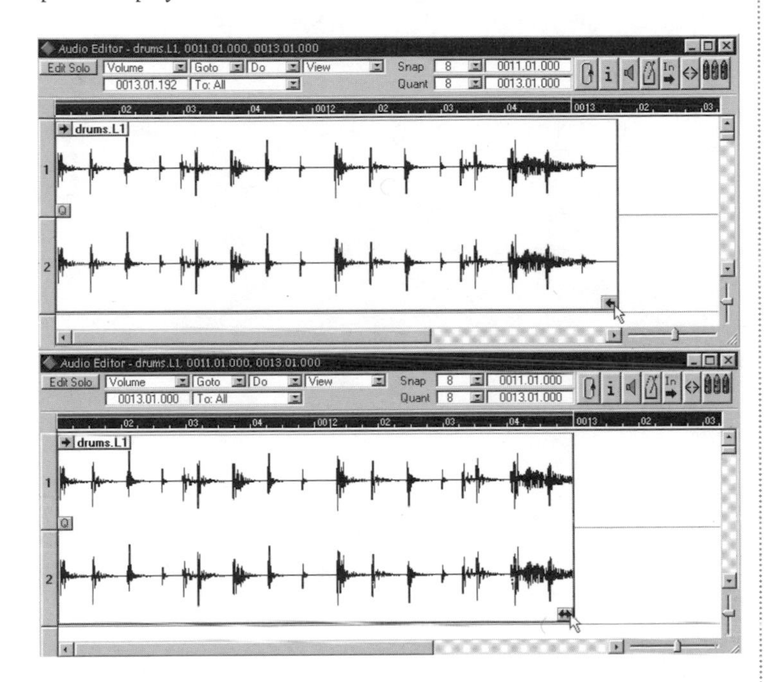

Figure 6.1: By dragging the handles in an audio event you can determine which part of the event plays.

Loops and zero-crossing points

If you want a section of audio to loop on playback, the first thing to do is to make sure the section has been recorded at exactly the correct tempo so when you play it back to back there are no gaps in between repeats and the end doesn't overlap the start.

The second thing is to make sure there are no clicks at the repeat point, and this may involve adjusting the start and/or end points by a minute amount. What you need to find are the zero crossing points.

If you zoom in on a waveform in an editor you will see it as a continuous wavy line which moves above and below a central

TIP

Many pieces of software have an option which automatically shifts cuts to the nearest zero crossing point. This is useful with any edit as it helps prevent clicks at the start and end of a cut

horizontal line. This line is the zero volume line and when the waveform is at that point has no volume.

If you try to form a loop at points where the waveform is above or below the line, they will have a volume, and unless they match perfectly, the result will be a click. So, the object of the exercise is to move the start and end points so they butt against each other on the zero crossing line when both have a volume of zero.

Many editors have a loop-finding function which lets you shuffle the end and start of the wave around and provides a visual indication of when the two sides match. Figure 6.2 shows how this works.

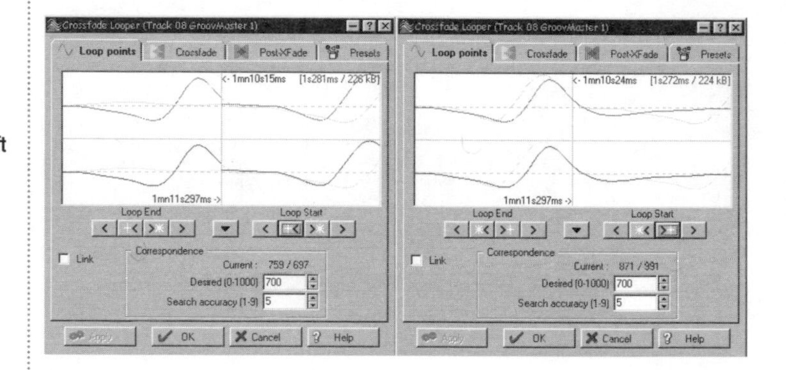

Figure 6.2: WaveLab's Crossfade Looper butts the end of the loop up against the start. The original setting on the left would cause a click. A little juggling produces the smoother click-free loop on the right.

Loop tips

When copying a sample loop in a sequencer's arrange window, use the sequencer's Snap To function to make sure the beginning of each copy sits right at the beginning of each bar. The Snap To function can usually be set to a division of the bar and ensures that any parts you move or copy always start on a specified bar division. Even if the loop is not quite the correct length, in most cases the fact that it restarts exactly at the beginning of each bar will gloss over any small discrepancies in its length.

If a loop is way too short or long, however, this won't work because the timing will drift out even in the space of one bar. In such cases you need to go back to the edit stage and edit it a little more accurately. Alternatively, you may need to change the length of the loop which you can do with the functions which are coming up next.

When using sample loops as the foundation for a song's backing, the easiest way to work is to record or import the loops into the sequencer and then set the sequencer's tempo to match the samples. You can then record other audio parts or MIDI parts at that tempo and everything will fit just fine.

QUICK LOOP TIP 1

Record the part you want to loop twice in succession and use the second recording for the loop. This ensures that the frequencies at the end of the loop or any reverb tails, for example, are present at the start of the loop. If you loop the first recording there will be no reverb, say, at the beginning so the reverb will sound cut off at the start of each loop.

If you want to add other samples, you must make sure they have been recorded at exactly the same tempo as the original ones otherwise they will not play in time. However, if that is the case, you can try the following...

Time stretching and pitch shifting

These are yet two more cool tricks that are easy to do with digital audio and which can't be done with a tape recording. Time stretching changes the duration of a part without changing the pitch. Pitch shifting changes the pitch without changing the duration. This is exactly what some loop-based software such as Acid, described in Chapter 5, does.

These functions are very useful for all manner of things such as changing a loop to make it fit a specific tempo, making a part match the pitch of another, and bringing a slightly out-of-tune recording back into pitch. You can even experiment with androgynous voices by lowering the pitch of a female voice or raising the pitch of a male voice.

If you need to change the pitch of a voice for musical purposes, make sure the software has a formant control. Formants are the tonal characteristics which make a voice male or female and if they are not compensated for during a vocal pitch shift you can end up with a vocal that sounds like Mickey Mouse.

Most audio software has time stretch and pitch shift functions built-in and is most cases it's simply a matter of selecting a new tempo or a pitch change and then letting the software do its stuff. These functions do have limits, however, and the further away from the original material that the process takes it, the more likely it is to add unwanted artefacts such as distortion.

Fades

You can create fade ins and outs in the mixer section of most software by manually adjusting the faders. However, you can create more accurate fades in many editors. Some let you create precision curves, perhaps specifying a linear or logarithmic curve, and the exact start and end point of the fades. With others you can draw in a curve directly onto the waveform.

If you need precision, use an editor. If you prefer a 'real feel' mix, use the faders in the mixer.

QUICK LOOP TIP 2

If you have a part you'd like to loop but which is proving stubbornly obstinate, copy a section from the start and merge it with the end of the part using a crossfade. This will make it easier to find a good loop point. Most editors have a 'merge with crossfade' function. If you're using a sequencer, place the section on a separate track at the end of the part, crossfade the two parts then merge the two tracks.

TIP

Crossfading is the process of fading out one section while fading in another. Again, most editors and sequencers have a function to help with this. If yours doesn't, overlap the two sections and create a fade out at the end of the first one and a fade in at the start of the second.

7

Processing and effects

Effects processing is yet another digital audio strong point. Most effects are applied during playback in real-time, often via a plug-in. This requires a certain amount of processing power and some systems give you the option of processing data 'off line' in case your system can't handle real-time processing.

Some functions, such as time stretching and pitch shifting, are usually handled off-line due to the amount of processing required. Like editing, effects processing is generally non-destructive although some off-line processes may alter the original material.

The range of effects available is legion, ranging from common and essential effects such as EQ and dynamics to the wild, weird and whacky

Effects software

Software check

- Hyperprism (Mac)
- T-RackS (PC, Mac, BeOS)
- ReCycle (PC and Mac)
- MetaSynth (Mac)

Most effects packages come in the form of plug-ins although there are a few stand-alone programs. Plug-ins are generally more flexible for processing individual tracks as you can apply effects to specific tracks and hear the result in the context of the mix. However, for processing an entire recording, a stand-alone effects pack may be preferred, and it is likely to require fewer resources than running a sequencer and plug-in effect together.

Into the effects category we could also add specialised processing software such as ReCycle which is an excellent tool for working with loops. It lets you chop up a loop, put the segments back in a different order, change drum sounds within the loop and change the tempo. MetaSynth is a sound generator which reads graphics images and generates audio files from them. Powerful and fascinating.

Plug-ins

Plug-ins are one of the great features of digital recording. As their name suggests they 'plug in' to the host recording software to provide additional features. Most plug-ins are effects processors but the range is vast – everything from EQ and reverb to vocoders and sonic enhancers. There are dozens of commercial plug-ins available and dozens of free ones, too, which can be downloaded from the Internet (see the Appendix for a list of some useful Web sites).

TIP

You must make sure that your host software is compatible with the type of plug-ins you want to use. On the PC this is not a problem as there is one main standard known as DirectX.

Most software also supports VST plug-ins. While this format was originally developed by Steinberg for use in its Cubase VST sequencer, it has now been accepted as a de facto standard by most developers.

VST plug-ins are the closest we have yet to a standard on the Apple Mac, with most software developers appearing keen to support it. Other Mac plug-in formats include Adobe Premier, Digidesign AudioSuite and Digidesign TDM. There are fewer Premier and AudioSuite plug-ins than VST plug-ins and the VST standard is generally accepted as being the best. TDM is really for use with Digidesign's high-end Pro Tools system and these plug-ins attract a heavy price premium.

EQ

EQ, short for equalisation, is the most widely used effect, and virtually all digital audio software has built-in EQ functions. EQ is used to cut or boost specific frequency bands in the audio and there are several types of EQ which do this is different ways.

EQ terms

There are five common EQ terms you need to understand.

Cutoff frequency or cutoff point This is the point at which the EQ kicks in. Depending upon the EQ type, frequencies above, below or either side of the cutoff-frequency may be affected.

Resonance This is also sometimes known as Q, bandwidth, emphasis or peak. It's the range of frequencies either side of the cutoff point. By increasing the resonance, the range of frequencies around the cutoff point narrows so if this was boosted, for example, there would be a peak in the frequency band, see Figure 7.1.

Software check

There are far too many plug-ins to single out a few so here's a list of the major plug-in developers:

AnTares

Arboretum

Cakewalk

Prosoniq

Sonic Foundry

Steinberg/ Spectral Design

TC Works

Waves

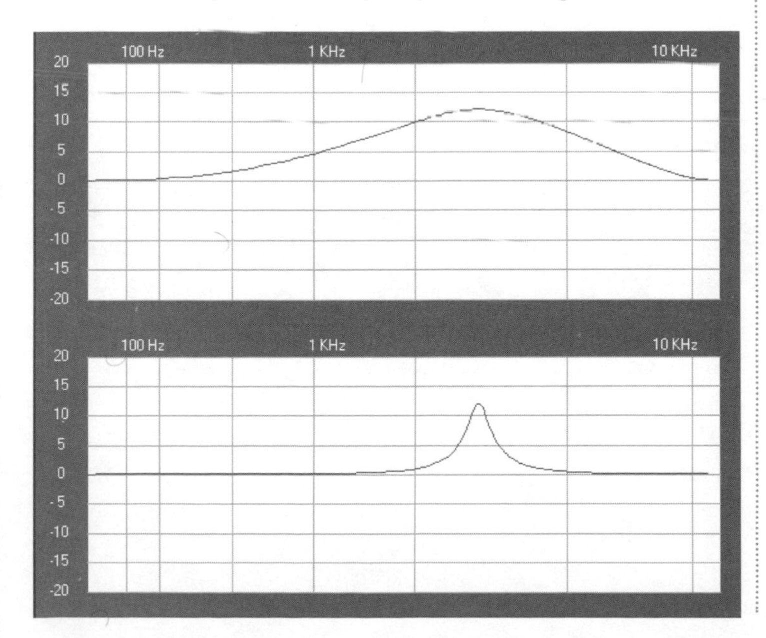

Figure 7.1: The top example shows a frequency boost with a very wide bandwidth. The lower example shows the result of narrowing it.

Attenuation Techy-type term for reduction, the opposite of amplification.

Roll-off or slope This is the rate at which the filter's effect increases as it moves further away from the cutoff point. It's usually measured in dB and the distance from the cutoff point, measured in octaves. A typical slope, therefore, will be quoted as 6dB/octave. You can see from Figure 7.2 that the 'stronger' curves have a greater filtering effect. If the roll-off of a filter is not given it will likely be 12dB/octave.

Figure 7.2 (7eq2): Three typical roll-off curves.

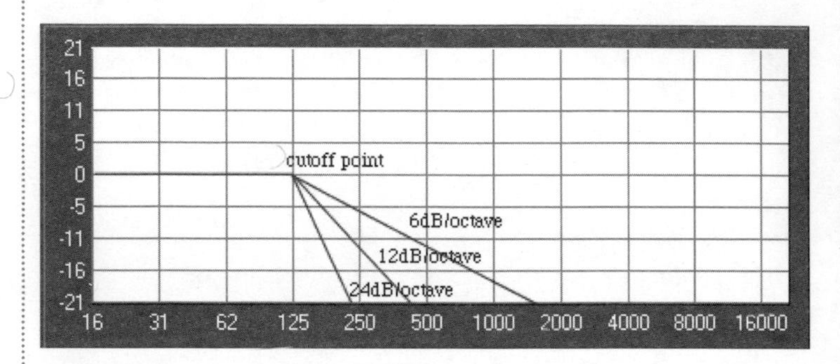

A higher roll-off curve does not necessarily make the filter better. If that were the case an 'ideal' filter would have a vertical slope but this would cut the frequencies dead at that point which would sound very unnatural indeed.

Gain This is a control which determines the amount by which a signal is cut (attenuated) or boosted.

Graphic EQ

There are two common types of EQ – graphic and parametric. A Graphic EQ (Figure 7.3) divides the frequency range into several bands which can individually be cut or boosted. Theoretically, the spectrum can be divided into any number of bands but common divisions are 5, 8 and 10.

It's common for the frequency of each band to be twice that of the preceding one. A doubling of the frequency represents a doubling of the octave so musically that's very useful. A graphic EQ is useful for shaping the overall tone of the sound.

INFO

Some developers call parametric EQ 'paragraphic EQ'

Parametric EQ

A parametric EQ (Figure 7.4) lets you specify the cutoff frequency you wish to process. It can, therefore, home in quite accurately on any part of the spectrum. They typically have three controls – cutoff

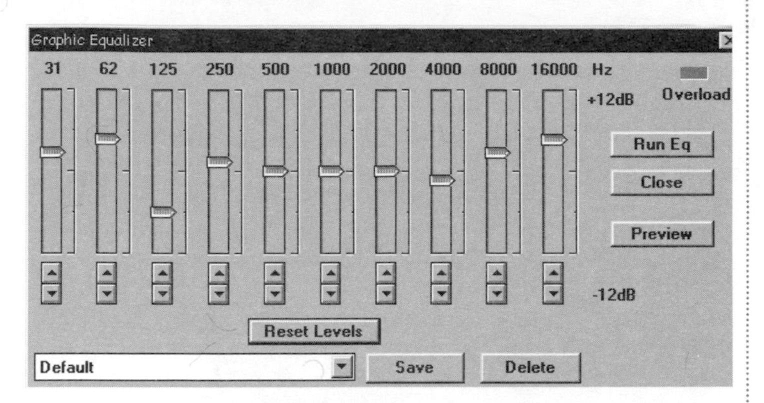

Figure 7.3: A graphic EQ divides the frequency spectrum into bands.

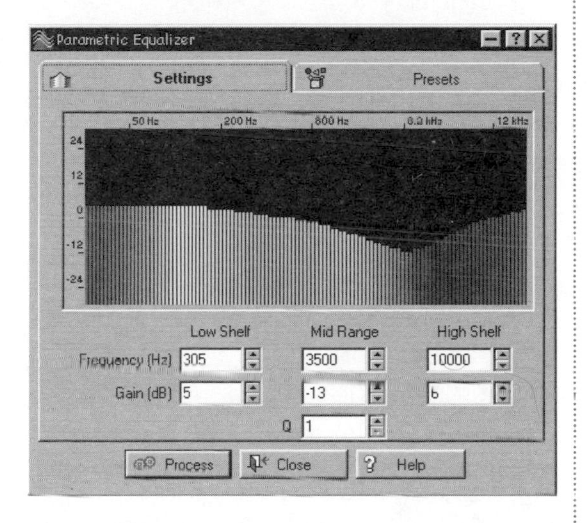

Figure 7.4: The parametric EQ in WaveLab has three bands and a nice graphic display to show exactly how the frequencies are being affected.

frequency, bandwidth and level – although some have additional features to make them more flexible. It's not uncommon to see a parametric EQ with more than one band.

Filters

The dividing line between an EQ and a filter is a thin one if, indeed, one still exists at all. Traditionally, EQ was used on devices such as mixers to help 'equalise' a recording – in other words to compensate for the deficiencies and inaccuracies of recording equipment. But that was in the early days of recording, and modern recording systems are extremely accurate. EQ is now used more as an effect in its own right rather than as a 'correctional facility'.

Filters are used in synthesisers to shape the tone of the sound.

As developers have produced more powerful and more specialised 'tone modification' software, they have borrowed features from one to include in the other, hence the blurring of boundaries.

There are six common filter types whose operation is fairly easy to understand.

Low pass This passes frequencies below the cutoff point while attenuating the higher ones. It's the most common filter type and the most natural as it removes high frequencies which are usually the first to go in most environments.

High pass The opposite of the low pass filter. It passes the high frequencies and attenuates the lower ones

High shelf Cuts or boosts the frequencies above the cutoff point.

Low shelf Cuts or boosts the frequencies below the cutoff point. Shelf filters are used to change a broad spectrum of the sound.

Band pass This removes frequencies either side of the cutoff point.

Band reject or notch The opposite of the band pass filter which attenuates frequencies around the cutoff point and passes the rest. Sometimes the two are combined into a filter which can cut or boost at the selected frequency.

EQ tips

If you're new to EQ, here are a few suggestions you might find useful as you ponder whether to cut, boost or leave well alone...

- To boost the bass, try the area around 80 – 120Hz for the low end and between 2 – 4kHz for the mid range.
- Use a paragraphic EQ or band filters to home in on a bass or snare drum, for example, to add some punch.
- Likewise, use these filters for reducing boomy bass areas.
- Use a high shelf filter to add sparkle by boosting the upper range.
- Our ears are naturally attuned to the 1 – 5kHz range so give this a little boost to add presence.
- Good EQing is not about boosting every frequency. If you do you'll simply end up with a louder version of the recording you had before. Be selective and if you want to balance a sound, try cutting unwanted frequencies instead of boosting the one you want want to accentuate.
- Boosting frequencies increases their amplitude which will increase the overall level of the recording. Watch out for this and make sure the output doesn't clip or distort.
- EQ is as much art as science so feel free to ignore any of these suggestions...

Dynamics

Dynamics effects are the most common effects after EQ and certainly some of the most useful. The most common dynamics effects are compression and limiting which both involve reducing the dynamic range of a signal. In other words (remembering what we learned in Chapter 2), they reduce the difference between the loudest and quietest parts.

This has several uses – to 'even out' a part where the volume levels vary wildly (vocals are a common source of this type of problem), to add punch to a part, and to prepare audio for broadcasting.

Dynamics controls

Most dynamics processors have five controls:

Threshold This is the level at which the effect kicks in. In most cases you want compression to start when the signal nears the upper end of its range.

Ratio This is the amount of compression applied. With a ratio of 2:1, for example, an increase in level of 2dB would be reduced to just 1dB. A limiter is basically a compressor with a very high ratio so that no matter how much louder a signal becomes, the output will be limited to a fixed level.

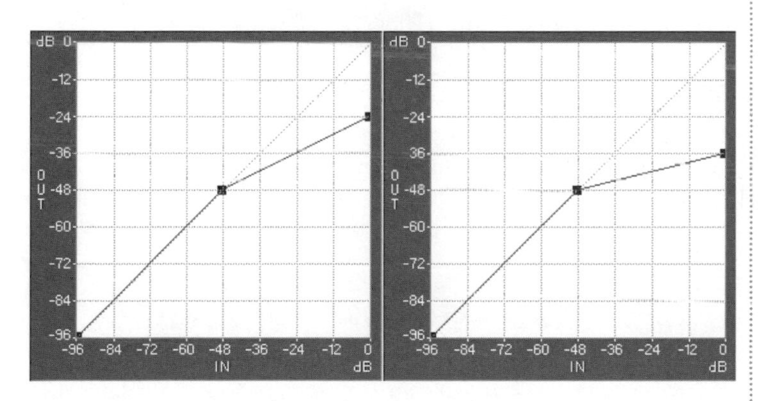

Figure 7.5: The differences between compression ratios of 2:1 (left) and 4:1 (right).

Attack This is the time it takes for the compressor to kick in after the signal hits the threshold level. If the attack time is too fast it can cut off the attack transient of percussive sounds such as drums. A slightly slower attack lets the punch through but still compresses the rest of the sound.

Release This is the time it takes for the compressor to stop compressing when the signal drops below the threshold level. If the signal is constantly above and below the threshold and the release is too fast, it can cause a pumping effect which is generally undesirable.

Gain Compression, by its nature, reduces the volume of a sound so most compressors have a volume adjustment to compensate.

Hard and soft knees

A 'hard knee' compressor applies the full compression effect as soon as the sound hits the threshold level. In some cases this can cause a pumping effect. 'Soft knee' compression applies the effect gradually as the signal moves further above the threshold level resulting in smoother changes.

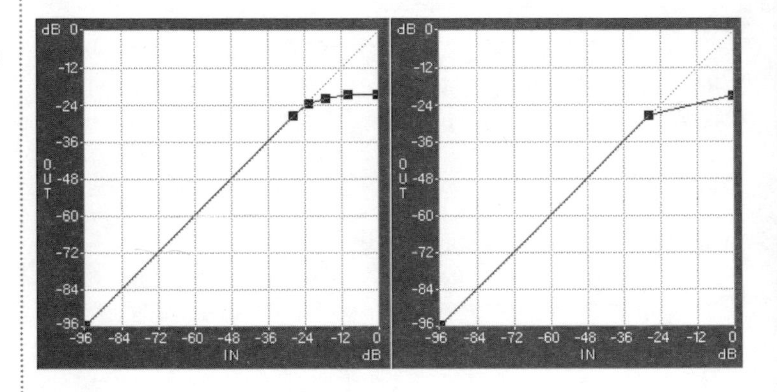

Figure 7.6: The difference between hard knee (right) and soft knee (left) compression.

De-esser

Speech and vocals contain sibilants which are S, T, CH and SH sounds and these are often exaggerated by recording producing a hissing sound. Thcy can be removed by various delicate combinations of filtering and compression but there are also dedicated processors which can help reduce or remove it.

DC offset

This is a simple but essential routine you should run on a part before creating a loop. In an editor, you'll notice that most waveforms sit fairly well balanced above and below a ventral horizontal 'zero volume' line. Occasionally, due to an equipment mismatch somewhere, the waveform may be offset a little higher or lower. This causes clicks on playback and makes it difficult to find silent zero crossing points (see Chapter 6) when creating loops. Most software includes this function.

Normalisation

This sounds like a neat function – it increases the volume of a part to the highest level it can go without becoming distorted. However, it is not a panacea for low-level recordings because if the recording contains noise then the noise will increase in level along with the main signal. Normalisation can be useful for making several parts a similar, maximum volume.

Noise reduction

If you do find some noise has made its way into a recording there are effects ready to try to remove it. Noise can take various forms and there are effects designed to remove the sort of clicks, pops and crackles you might find when recording from vinyl. In fact, there are several pieces of software designed specifically to help you transfer material from vinyl to CD, improving and enhancing it as you go.

Other forms of noise are present in the background of a recording and some specialist processing functions seek to remove this in a clever way. You need a section of the recording which contains just the unwanted noise and nothing else. The software analyses this, making a noise print of it, and then removes it from the main body of the recording.

Loudness maximisers

In most forms of recording, particularly music, there's a continual effort to get 'more sound' into the system, to make it punchier, more exciting and to add sparkle. This can be done by the judicious use of compression, limiting, EQ and resampling, but there are also dedicated all-in-one effects designed to make a recording sound bigger, fuller, louder and more up-front.

Most of these are easy to use, it generally being a case of twiddling a few dials and listening to the result. Some of them are very clever and do, indeed, add a few more dB to the perceived output.

Reverb

Reverb is used to add ambience to a sound, and our ears use the reverb effect to tell us the sort of environment the sound was recorded in. A very dry sound, for example, suggests it was recorded in a small room with very absorbent surfaces while a sound with a lot of reverberation suggests a large area such as a concert hall or a cathedral.

There are probably over a dozen software-based digital reverb effects. However, as you might imagine, modern effects often add a new dimension to the traditional process. Some reverb effects such as Cakewalk's Audio FX3 Soundstage, let you define the size and shape of the room. Others such as Sonic Foundry's Acoustic Mirror, impart an acoustic signature to a sound as if it had been recorded in a specific environment such as a concert hall, a stairwell or under a bridge.

Most digital audio software has at least one built-in reverb effect although some are better than others. But if your software has built-in reverb, do explore it thoroughly before you look at other options because it might well do all you need.

The main thing to remember about using reverb is not to add too much. Even a small amount can lift an otherwise dry sound. Be careful not to overdo reverb on drums or it can sound as if they were recorded in a warehouse. However, many smart effects have been created by adding reverb to just the snare drum (this, of course, requires that the snare was recorded separately). But still, use with caution.

Delay

Delay or echo has been traditionally used to add repeats to a sound. It can also be used effectively with certain sounds as a reverb substitute. Try it with vocals for example.

Some of the more sophisticated effects feature a multi-tap delay which lets you specify different delay times, strengths and repetitions for each delay.

Delay (and even reverb) can be used to create a pseudo stereo effect from a mono signal by panning the dry signal to one side of the stereo image and the delayed signal to the other side. Try this with a very short delay time or a dry reverb.

It will come as no surprise to learn that there are stereo enhancers, effects which can broaden the width of the stereo image and create 3D effects. Take a look at Wave's S1 Stereo Imager and Steinberg's Ambisone.

Chorus, phasing and flanging

These effects may seem to produce similar results but they are different as you can tell if you listen closely, and the effects are achieved in different ways. However, it's convenient to deal with them together as they all add a degree of thickening and motion to a sound.

Chorus is the traditional 'thickener' and created using a short delay with modulation of the pitch. It is often used with vocals to give the impression that more than one voice is singing, however it can equally well be used with other sounds. Some chorus effects let you specify the number of voices and can even create harmonies.

Flanging is similar to chorus but it uses shorter delays and feeds the signal back on itself.

Phasing uses even shorter delay times but little feedback which results in a more subtle sound.

Phasing and flanging can be used with vocals but is more commonly used with instrument sounds

Overdrive and distortion

There are many ways to distort a signal as you'll soon find out on your journey through digital recording! However, sometimes this type of effect is part of a sound, particularly with guitar lines. Overdrive was originally created by overloading a guitar amp to the point of clipping (see Chapter 3), an effect much beloved by heavy metal bands.

Using such effects it's possible to record a guitar line straight and then experiment with the degree and type of distortion effect you want to apply to it.

Sample conversion

If you need to reduce the sample rate or resolution for compatibility with another system or project, you want to make sure that the change maintains the highest audio quality possible. This is also true if you're working at 24-bit or a higher rate than 44.1kHz and need to reduce this to 'CD quality' for burning to a CD. Incidentally, all things being equal, this will produce a better quality recording than using 16-bit recording throughout the creation of the project.

Without getting too far into the nitty gritty, there are a number of ways of reducing the number of bits in a recording. The most efficient is dithering which, believe it or not, actually adds low-level noise to a recording before reducing the number of bits. Trust us on this one – it works! There are also high-end conversion systems designed particularly for pro use.

INFO

See Chapter 3 for more about sample rate and resolution

The weird and wonderful

There's not much you can't do with a digital signal and here are just a few of the more interesting digital audio processing functions and effects which are out there.

Vocoder Creates vocoder-type effects from the audio.

Lo fi Designed to put back the noise, hiss and crackles you were so careful to keep out.

Analogue tape simulator Applies the tape saturation and overdrive effects which were possible with tape recording.

Tube amp simulator Simulates the warmth and recording characteristics of tube-driven amplifiers.

Microphone simulator Makes a sound appear to have been recorded by one of a number of different microphones.

Stereo imaging Increases the spread of the stereo image making it appear wider than the speakers.

No round-up of digital effects would be complete without mentioning Cycling 74's Pluggo, a collection of over 74 VST-compatible plug-ins featuring everything from 'traditional' effects to granulation, a type of cut-it-up-and-put-it-back-together synthesis.

Mixing and mastering

When you've recorded all the tracks for a song, processed them and applied effects, the last step is to mix them down to a stereo file – the 'master'. If you can bear it, don't listen to the recording for a few days before doing the mix. There is a recognised phenomenon called ear fatigue, and if you've spent a few days listening to the same piece, your ears may be dull to certain frequencies.

Speakers

The object of the mix is to make the recording sound as good as it possibly can on all types of speakers. This is a bit of a no-win situation and you'll know yourself how different a CD sounds when played on your hi fi, on a walkman and on the car stereo.

It will help if you have a set of professional monitor speakers. Do not try to use computer speakers, it will end in disaster.

Harmonic spread

Music can contain frequencies which run right through the audible spectrum, rather like an orchestra which contains instruments ranging from the lows of the bass tuba to the highs of the piccolo. You don't have to fill the spectrum quite as completely as that but a broad range will give the ear something to listen to at all points.

One of the most sensitive areas is the frequency range between 1 and 5kHz which is where speech falls, and our ears are naturally attuned to it. It can be tempting to push all sounds into this band, perhaps adding, say, a synth line in this range if you are looking for another sound to fill out the music. However, if you cram too many sounds here the individual sounds will be indistinct and you will lose the very clarity you were seeking in the first place.

So the message is, spread the sounds around throughout the frequency spectrum, don't put them all in once place. And try to balance them so there are highs as well as a bass content otherwise it will still sound out of balance. You can easily prove this by putting on one of your favourite records and then turning up the bass and turning down the treble and then do the reverse.

Stereo positioning

When starting a mix, set all pan controls to a central position. Some people work on getting a reasonably good sound and mix before panning tracks while others seem to pan as they go.

Stereo positioning is related to harmonic content so often you have to juggle pan positions and EQ at the same time. Generally, vocals are positioned in the middle of the mix. It's also common to leave the bass in the middle and often the drums, too. Our ears find

INFO

Many studios use a cheap pair of car speakers reasoning that if it sounds good on those and on monitors, it must be a good mix!

TIP

After doing a mix, play it on as many different systems as you can and you'll soon discover if there are any areas that your mixing and monitoring system is cutting or boosting.

TIP

Before starting a mix, set all the EQ controls to their central position.

TIP

If you want clarity and separation between sounds containing similar frequencies then place them at different points in the stereo image.

it more difficult to detect the position of lower frequencies so even if you panned the bass guitar slightly to the left, your ears would still probably think it was in the middle. So most people leave it there!

If recording a band-type line-up, you could pan each instrument to the position it would occupy on stage. That usually means vocals and drums in the middle and the other performers at their allotted spots. But do remember the bass effect and even though the bass player may be a foot from the left of the stage, panning the instrument there is generally not a good idea.

If the drums have been recorded live then some stereo separation will give them a sense of depth and proportion. However, you can do really neat things if the drums have been recorded individually or if you are using a MIDI or sample-based drum track. For example, if there's a three-tom roll around the kit, try putting the toms at different positions in the stereo image. If the part includes a pattern played on bongos or congas, panning them to the left and right will not only separate them but create an interesting rhythmic counterplay across the stereo image. Note that it's usual to put the bass drum and snare in the centre so as not to overbalance the mix.

ReWire

We mentioned ReWire in Chapter 5. It's a system for routing the audio from soft synths through the host sequencer's audio mixer, allowing effects and EQ to be applied to it and, if the sequencer supports mixer automation, these channels can be automated, too.

ReWire brings additional sounds within the one mixing environment which makes the entire song easier to mix. If you have a choice, selecting software which supports ReWire – assuming your host sequencer does – will simplify the mixing process and give you more control over it, too.

Mixer automation

Even if you haven't been inside a professional recording studio, you will doubtless have seen giant mixing desks with countless numbers of channels on TV. Each of the channels controls a track, and it's the job of the engineer or producer to adjust them so they all balance superbly. Not an easy task if you only have two hands.

Thanks goodness for mixer automation then, which remembers the positions and movements of the controls during mixdown and automatically moves them during playback. It allows the engineer to concentrate on small sections of the mix each time through the recording.

Automated mixers are expensive. The good news is that most sequencers include a mixer automation feature. The mixer will typically have a Record or Write button and during playback it will remember any adjustments you made to the controls. This is incredibly useful for all sorts of things, of course. It can help you create a dynamic mix, compensating for a part which has been recorded with uneven volume levels (how did that happen, then?) but it can also be used to fade instruments in and out and to create dynamic panning effects – but use this carefully and not with the vocal!

Mixing MIDI and audio data

Many musicians record using a combination of MIDI and audio, often creating the backing tracks with MIDI and then recording vocals and perhaps an acoustic guitar or a sax. How to mix these into one final stereo part? This depends on what you are mixing down to. If you are mixing to a DAT machine, for example, then you can do the mix in the sequencer's mixer and route the audio from the computer and external mixer (if you are using external MIDI sound modules) to the DAT.

However, if you want to record the final mix as a digital audio file to hard disk you must first convert the MIDI data into audio data. How easy this is will depend you your system but whatever you have and however you do it, one thing remains the same – the MIDI data must be recorded as audio data.

If you are using the MIDI sounds built into a soundcard it may appear as though the MIDI parts and the audio parts are coming from the same place (they aren't, they just meet up at the soundcard's audio output) and you may wonder if there is a magic button you can press which will convert the MIDI recordings to audio. Generally there is not although some systems do make the conversion very easy.

With other systems, you need to channel the MIDI parts into the audio in socket of the soundcard. If you are using external MIDI equipment, simply connect their output to the card's input.

If you are using a card with on-board MIDI sounds, the most straightforward way is to connect the soundcard's audio out to its audio in. Do make sure to mute any audio tracks during recording otherwise they will be recorded, too.

However, many soundcards come with a software mixer which may allow you to use the MIDI output as a recording source. If you can do this, it removes the digital-to-analogue-to-digital conversion stage which results in better quality audio. However, sometimes this can be a little tricky to set up, again, depending on the system so, as usual, read the instructions, both the manual and any on-line documentation, carefully. Once the MIDI data has been recorded as

TIP

Yamaha's SW1000XG soundcard and its accompanying XGWorks software have a facility which routes the MIDI parts through the system and converts them to digital audio.

TIP

Many an album has sold on the strength of its cover so do not underestimate the importance of the artwork. Even when submitting a demo CD, a good cover, even if a little rough, can be beneficial. If you are running off your own CDs to sell at gigs, it's worth spending a little time, money and effort on the packaging so your fans are getting a quality product.

audio, it can be loaded into audio tracks and the entire song mixed and bounced down to a stereo file.

In good order

Give careful thought to the order of the songs. Do you want the strongest song first or last? Do you want to alternate the up-tempo songs with the slower ones or do you want them grouped together? It may help reduce ear fatigue if consecutive songs are not in the same key.

A mastering house or DIY?

If you use a good mastering house to master your recording professionally, it will assemble the songs in whatever order you wish so that's not something you must do at the mixing stage. It will also check that the fades are constant, the level right, the gaps between the tracks correct, and spot any problems in your recording which you may not be aware of. Their equipment will be better than yours so any adjustments they make should be top quality.

If you're quite confident about your mixing abilities then you may prefer to create your own 'master' which you can give to a pressing plant for duplication. Once upon a time, a DAT tape was the medium of choice for this but most companies now also accept CD masters.

Burning audio CDs

To create – or burn, in the vernacular – an audio CD you need, of course, a CD-R drive – these are now very inexpensive. Most drives come bundled with software which will do the job. The process is pretty automatic and usually consists of little more than dragging the audio files into a playlist window.

If you want to do 'clever stuff' such as changing the size of the gap or pause between tracks or enter sub-index information then you may need a piece of software dedicated to creating audio CDs.

Disk-at-once vs track-at-once

These are the two ways of writing an audio CD. In Track-at-once (TAO) mode, short pieces of housekeeping data are written before and after each track. These can create a click when played back on a music CD player (as opposed to a CD ROM drive). Also, with TAO you don't have control over the inter-track gaps. Some older CD-Rs can only write in this mode. In Disc-at-once mode, the entire disc is written in one go. This gives you far more control over the layout, you can fiddle with the inter-track gaps and the CD won't click on audio CD players. So this is the mode to use every time.

9

MP3

If you have an interest in music you will almost certainly have heard of MP3s. They have revolutionised the distribution of music over the Internet, given record companies nightmares and led to more than a few law suits being dropped on sites distributing MP3 files.

What is MP3?

MP3 is short for MPEG 3. Helpful, eh? MPEG stands for Moving Picture Experts Group which gave its name to a range of standards used in coding video and audio data. MP3 is just such a standard for compressing audio data. When you consider that a one-minute 'CD quality' file is around 10Mb in size you can see that it's totally impracticable to send even one song to someone via email or to download it from the Internet. At least until we all have high-speed Internet connections.

MP3 can compress an audio file making it up to 80 times smaller. However, MP3 is a 'lossy' codec which means it discards information in order to reduce the file size. And it has to throw away a lot of information to reduce the file by a factor of 80. Reducing it to 12 times its size, however, retains most of the essential information and, indeed, many people claim this is as near CD quality as makes no difference. Others would argue the point. The important thing is that it's still 'good' quality which most people are happy to listen to.

With MP3 you can store maybe 12 or 14 hour's worth of music on a CD and you can choose from a range of dozens of portable MP3 players which can store and play MP3 files downloaded from your computer.

It's important to realise than MP3 files are data files and not audio files. You can write them to a CD but they will not play on an audio CD player. You must play them via a computer, although some enterprising manufacturers have released audio CD players which also play MP3 files.

Really dumb thing

If the companies had had the foresight to recognise the potential of MP3 they could have turned it to their advantage in many ways, not least of all as new means of music distribution. In fact, this is very likely to happen but there has already been a lot of blood, sweat, tears, and much money wasted

The furore

MP3 has given record companies headaches because people have been converting albums into MP3 format and distributing them illegally on the Web. Naturally, they are very upset (putting it mildly) which has led to law suits flying all over the place trying to prevent this.

The future of MP3

The digital revolution will not disappear. However, when the record companies get their act together the emphasis may move away from MP3 files to another compressed audio format, one which can be copy-protected and controlled.

However, trying to make listeners change from MP3 files to a less open format will not be easy, particularly as many have already invested heavily in the format by way of software and MP3 players. And already many famous acts are putting MP3 files on the Web for downloading either free of charge or for a small sum.

TIP

No one knows what will happen so if you get involved with distributing music over the Web, make sure you keep up with new developments.

Creating MP3 files

MP3 is simply another data format. Most of the major audio programs now include an option to encode a recording as an MP3 file, and there are dozens of programs on the Web which can do it.

There is a decision you have to make which is whether to use a constant bit rate (CBR) or a variable bit rate (VBR). The more bits you use, the higher the quality (you'll know this from Chapter 3) but the larger the file will be. Most people find 128kbps a good compromise but if the files are for your own use and you have plenty of disk space, try 256kbps. On the other hand, if listening to the files through earphones with an MP3 player, you may find 64kbps okay.

VBR adjusts the number of bits used according to the complexity of the material. It can, therefore, make the files smaller without detracting from the quality. The disadvantage is that some MP3 players cannot calculate VBR-encoded song lengths correctly.

Putting your music on the Web

MP3 files are a great way to send your music to friends, but you can go a step further and put them on a Web site where everyone can access them.

Visitors can download complete MP3 files but they can also be streamed which means they start to play almost immediately someone accesses them. This is obviously more immediate but it does mean you need to be circumspect with the file size. Even though many people now have a 56K modem, their fastest connection speed is likely to be around 48K and to cater for visitors who may be using a slower modem you should be thinking in terms of 28K. You can also save space by using mono rather than stereo files.

INFO

Many sites now include lo rate and hi rate files so visitors can choose. They can stream the lo rate file and, if they like it, download the hi rate file.

Appendix – useful Web sites

Software and hardware

Adaptec – www.adaptec.com
AnTares – www.antares-systems.com
Apogee Electronics – www.apogeedigital.com
Arboretum – www.arboretum.com
Bias – www.bias-inc.com
BitHeadz – www.bitheadz.com
Cakewalk – www.cakewalk.com
Creative Labs – www.creaf.com
CreamWare – www.creamware.de/index_e.htm
Cycling '74 – www.cycling74.com
David Brown's Plug-ins – www.db-audioware.com
Digital Audio Labs – www.digitalaudio.com
Digidesign – www.digidesign.com
Emagic – www.emagic.de
fxpansion – www.fxpansion.com
Guillemot – www.guillemot.com
Harmony Central – www.harmony-central.com
Innovative Quality Software – www.iqsoft.com
Koblo – www.koblo.com
Mark of the Unicorn – www.motu.com
Mixman – www.mixman.com
Native Instruments – www.native instruments.com
Propellerheads – www.propellerheads.se
Prosoniq – www.prosoniq.com
Seer Systems – www.seersystems.com
SEK'D – www.sekd.com
Shareware Music machine – www.hitsquad.com
Sonic Foundry – www.sfoundry.com
Steinberg – www.steinberg.net dialspace.dial.pipex.com/town/road/gbp97
Syntrillium – www.syntrillium.com
TC Works – www.tcworks.de
Voyetra, Turtle Beach – www.voyetra-turtle-beach.com
U&I Software – www.uisoftware.com
Waves – www.waves.com
Yamaha – www.yamaha.co.uk – www.xgfactory.com

CD

CD-ROM Digital Audio – www.tardis.ed.ac.uk/~psyche/cdda/
Digital Domain – www.digido.com/Digital Sound Page
http://digitalsoundpage.com

Organisations

APRS (Association of Professional Recording Services) – www.aprs.co.uk
BPI – British Phonographic Industry – www.bpi.co.uk
MCPS (MechanicalCopyright Protection Society) – www.mcps.co.uk
Musicians' Union – www.musiciansunion.org.uk
PRS (Performing Right Society) – www.prs.co.uk/index.html
RIAA (Recording Industry Association of America) – www.riaa.com

Magazines and publishers

Computer Music – www.computermusic.co.uk
Future Publishing – www.futurenet.com
Music & Computers – www.music-and-computers.com
PC Publishing – www.pc-publishing.co.uk
SOS – www.sospubs.co.uk

MP3

BeSonic – www.besonic.com
MP3.com – www.mp3.com
peoplesound.com – www.peoplesound.com

Index